*Merry Christmas from*

. . . From Maidstone United.

. . . From Oxford United.

season's greetings

. . . From Tottenham Hotspur.

. . . From Kilmarnock.

*Merry Christmas*

. . . From Brighton.

. . . From Norwich City.

10655857

# THE TOPICAL TIMES
# FOOTBALL
# BOOK
## CONTENTS

# NEVER LOOK BACK!

## That's the motto of Tottenham Hotspur's RICHARD GOUGH

⚽ IT doesn't pay to look back too much in football, or think of 'what might have been'. If I did I could consider how the club I had just left went on to the UEFA Cup Final last season, and the club that I first wanted to join became Scottish Premier Division Champions.

But I'm not the type to have second thoughts, or worry about what has happened in the past. I live for the present, and think about the future. So it's of no concern to me that my previous club, Dundee United, reached the UEFA Cup Final in the season that I quit Tannadice.

In fact, I was highly delighted for the club, the players and the fans, and I made the trip to Dundee to watch the second leg against Gothenburg.

Similarly I was pleased that Glasgow Rangers, the club I was desperate to join at one stage, won the Scottish Championship in Graeme Souness' first season as player-manager.

Those successes didn't make me feel the slightest bit envious, because I look on the positive side of every situation. And I ended last season knowing I had advanced my career in every way by joining Tottenham Hotspur — particularly as we reached the F.A. Cup Final at Wembley!

Even if Spurs had not had that success, I would still be content with my decision to join the London club, because I feel Spurs are going to be a big force in the game in the next few years.

I had been happy with Dundee United, but I'd reached the stage where I felt I needed to better myself. United couldn't match the kind of terms I wanted, and so I had to move on.

Glasgow Rangers then made an offer, and I badly wanted to join them. It soon became clear, however, that Dundee United wouldn't sell me to Rangers or any other Scottish club.

But when Spurs and Chelsea came up with offers of £750,000 to match United's valuation, it was then down to me. I planned to fly down on a Monday morning, and talk to Spurs first, then go on to Chelsea. I was to make up my mind after seeing both clubs.

But as soon as I arrived at Spurs and met chairman Irving Scholar and manager David Pleat, there was no doubt in my mind that this was the club for me.

My reasons for leaving Dundee United were mainly financial. But I agreed to sign for Spurs before even starting to talk about personal terms. That's how sure I was that it was the right move.

6

Nothing that's happened since has made me change my mind. Spurs are a big club. They are always going to have a chance of winning honours — and that's really what it's all about.

When I joined Spurs, goalkeeper Ray Clemence was captain, and I expected him to remain in charge for as long as he was at White Hart Lane. But then Ray was injured and the manager asked me to lead out the side. A few weeks later he asked me to take over as regular skipper. I was surprised and honoured to be given the job.

I thought it was a nice touch to play my first match as skipper against Charlton Athletic, because they were my first club in Britain. Unfortunately, it wasn't a happy time for me. I came from my home in South Africa at the age of 16 to try my luck at the Valley.

But I was so lonely and homesick in my 'digs' near the ground that I went back home after seven months. I tried again with Dundee United when I was a little more mature, and this time it worked out well.

Perhaps I felt more at ease in Scotland. My father, Charlie, is a Scot. He was a paratrooper in the army, and was stationed in Sweden when I was born. He was a good enough footballer to captain the British Army team, and Charlton Athletic bought him out of the army to sign professional — as a centre-half.

My father didn't quite make the grade at the Valley, and Eddie Firmani, the South African who was a big star at Charlton, and for a spell in Italy, persuaded him to go out to Johannesburg.

The family settled out there when I was three years old and I learned the game playing for clubs in Southern Transvaal. I also played rugby at school, but I loved soccer more, and was only interested in becoming a professional footballer.

As a youngster with Dundee United I was a centre-half. But the central defence places in the first team were held down by the well-established pairing of David Narey and Paul Hegarty

There was no way I could get into the side in the centre of the defence, so I switched to full-back. Once I got into the team I stayed in, and went on to win Scottish caps in the position.

But at the back of my mind was always the thought that sooner or later I would want to revert to central defence. Spurs gave me that chance.

It couldn't have been a much bigger challenge for me at the start of last season. A new position, with a new club, in a new league — and with a very big transfer fee to justify.

But that's the kind of situation which brings the best out of me. I settled in quickly and it wasn't long before I was feeling very comfortable alongside Gary Mabbutt in the centre of the Spurs defence.

We are a little bit similar in that neither of us likes to just thump the ball away. We try to use it to bring our skilful players into the game.

Gary and I are both quite quick, and although we are not particularly tall, we can get up reasonably well for the high ball. I enjoy playing with him.

It was a surprise to me to discover that the English First Division is not as physically tough as the Scottish Premier Division.

It's a very demanding division in England, but not as physical as in Scotland. It's demanding because of the greater number of good sides, which means there are no easy matches.

In Scotland there are four or five good sides, but then a fair gap in standard. In England, although the top four are ahead of the rest, there is less difference between the top teams and the average sides.

And there is a great diversity of styles. A lot of teams play the long ball game, such as Wimbledon, Sheffield Wednesday and Watford, while others play a short-passing game.

I wouldn't say that one style was any better than the other. Teams have to play to their strengths and make the most of the players they've got.

It would be crazy for us at Spurs to play a long ball game because we have small, mobile forwards.

Our game is a complicated one involving short passing and a lot of movement. It suits us, and is successful.

But Arsenal last season had a lot of success playing a long ball game, using the height of Niall Quinn to advantage.

It's that difference in styles which makes the First Division so interesting. You can never relax because each opponent poses different problems. It's up to you to counteract them.

I believe we have a squad of players at Spurs who can match anything the other clubs can produce. I'm really looking forward to the next few years at White Hart Lane.

# MY IDOL

## ALAN IRVINE
### (Liverpool)

"My move from Falkirk to Liverpool last season gave me the chance to work with a boyhood idol — Liverpool player-manager Kenny Dalglish.

"When I was young I used to watch him play for Celtic, and he has always been my favourite player. But I'd never met him until I came down to Merseyside for my trial.

"Dundee and Dundee United were also interested in signing me, but once Liverpool made me an offer, I had no doubt where my future lay.

"I can learn so much from watching somebody like Kenny, but that's the case with all the first team here."

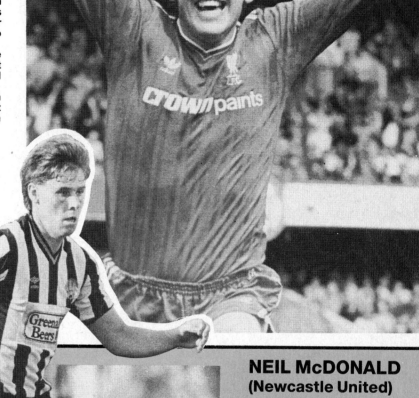

## NEIL McDONALD
### (Newcastle United)

Ask Newcastle United's Neil McDonald who his boyhood hero was and you hardly have time to complete the question before the England under-21 international fires off the name — Billy Bremner!

The Tyneside youngster idolised the former Leeds United and Scotland skipper so much that his proudest possessions as a kid were two footballer 'models' he painted to resemble the now Elland Road manager.

"For me, Billy will always be the player who has inspired me most when it comes to my own ambitions in the game," explains Neil.

"It was his sheer determination, enthusiasm and commitment to the game during the glory days of Leeds that first attracted me to him.

"In my eyes he was everything I wanted to become as a footballer, given the chance. He wasn't just a great player, but an inspiring leader who never knew the word defeat.

"It seemed only natural that when I was a kid and someone gave me two

## IAN ANDREWS
## (Leicester City)

"I come from Nottingham and was signed by Forest as a schoolboy. That meant I was lucky enough to have a few goalkeeping sessions with Peter Shilton. I took in his every word and action.

"On matchdays I'd stand behind the goal at the City ground, studying all aspects of his performance.

"Most keepers in League football are good shot-stoppers, but Shilton's all-round game was exceptional.

"From my vantage point I gained a shrewd knowledge of his reading of the game, his command of the goal area, the confidence and ease with which he dealt with crosses, and even the way he shouted at defenders."

## LEE DIXON
## (Stoke City)

"As a kid I was a striker or midfielder and Colin Bell of Manchester City was always the man I admired most. But on being converted to a full back while I was at Burnley, I began to think about the best players in the country in my new position.

"Top of my list was Mick Mills, then an England regular. His achievements in the game made him someone to respect.

"At the start of last season he signed me for his first club as a boss — Stoke City. And I began to see at first hand just what he knew about playing at full back.

"He has taught me so much since. You can still see in training all the assets that made him so successful. He has the vision to play the sort of pass I'd never dream of hitting.

"He has worked very hard on the defensive side of my play, making me a much better all-round player. It has been marvellous to play under someone who knows so much about the job I do".

## PAUL MOULDEN
## (Manchester City)

"Former Maine Road favourite Trevor Francis was my boyhood hero. It was marvellous that he was still at the club when I signed on schoolboy forms for City.

"I used to watch him closely in training whenever possible and studied him during matches. I recall one game against Leeds United when he tore them apart single-handed. It was a brilliant solo performance.

"I suppose I took to him because like me he was a goalscorer and I like to shield the ball the way he did. I haven't his pace, but I'm a similar type of player. I learned a lot watching Trevor.

"It was great for a young kid like me to see his idol at such close quarters."

model footballers I painted them to look like Billy.

"I well remember colouring in the very red hair, the white strip of Leeds and, of course, the number four on the back of the jersey. Every now and then I'd also do a touch-up job just to make sure the models remained smart!"

It wasn't until Neil was, in fact, establishing himself in the Newcastle line-up that he first got the opportunity to meet his 'hero' face to face.

"It had always been one of my ambitions," Neil reveals. "But, of course, Billy had retired from the playing side before I got going.

"Two or three years back, however, we were travelling to play a match against Nottingham Forest. Jack Charlton was our manager and I knew he was going to take in a match at Doncaster on his way there.

"As I wasn't going to be in the side for the Forest game, I asked Jack if I could travel over to Doncaster with him — just to meet Billy.

"Even though I was 18 or 19 at the time I still remember quaking in my shoes with excitement when Jack introduced us. That might sound daft, but it just about sums up how much I'd idolised him."

TREVOR FRANCIS

PETER SHILTON
*Southampton*

10

# PROGRAMMED FOR SUCCESS

Mark Lawrenson has played more than 500 games in a career that took in Preston North End and Brighton before a £900,000 move landed him at Liverpool in the summer of 1981.

He has appeared in two European Cup Finals, won an FA Cup medal, picked up three winners medals for the League Cup, won four League Championship medals and has been capped thirty-odd times by the Republic of Ireland.

And Mark has a souvenir from every single match. Tucked away in his Southport home, is a huge collection of programmes. Read on to see how this collection illustrates the highlights and set-backs that have been a feature of Mark's career.

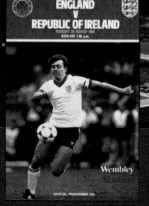

# MILESTONES THAT MEAN SO MUCH TO MARK LAWRENSON

### April 22, 1975
### Preston v. Watford

It's a rainy Tuesday night and the Deepdale pitch is a quagmire. I'm selected by manager Bobby Charlton to play right back in my first team debut. I'm up against winger Bobby Downes and I just try to stick to him like glue. It isn't a very eventful debut. We draw 2-2 and I do nothing wrong, nothing sensational. But I'm on my way.

### April 29, 1975
### Charlton v. Preston

My first 'big' game. Nearly 25,000 fans are at the Valley because the home team need to win to gain promotion. We take the lead but Charlton equalise with a disputed penalty. Then I'm involved in two incidents which help them win the match and achieve promotion to Division Two.

I head one goal-bound effort off the line and over the bar. Yet the referee awards a goal. Total injustice. Then, after chasing a through ball with Derek Hales, I fail to clear and he sticks it away for number three.

### August 29, 1976
### Preston Reserves v. Burnley Reserves

A new manager, Harry Catterick, is appointed after Bobby Charlton's resignation. The first club match he watches is a Central League game in which I'm playing.

Unfortunately, I tear my knee ligaments after 30 minutes and get carried off. The boss comes to see me in the dressing room and tells me, "If you hadn't been injured, you would have been in the first team on Saturday."

I'm out for three months but as soon as I'm fit, the manager makes good his promise.

### December 17, 1976
### Preston v. Shrewsbury Town

My first-ever goal in League football. Operating as a central defender, I go up for a corner and find the net with a diving header. It's our first in a 2-1 win.

### April 24, 1977
### Eire v. Poland

My international debut. Only 19 and I'm selected for a friendly with Poland at Dalymount Park. I was born in Preston, but my mother is Irish which means I'm eligible for the Republic.

I play for Preston on the Saturday, win my first cap on Sunday — and am playing again for my club on the Tuesday. A tiring schedule, but I'm on such a high I don't feel any strain.

### August 20, 1977
### Southampton v. Brighton

Brighton sign me while I'm on my summer holidays in Benidorm. Chairman Mike Bamber and I seal the deal over beans on toast in a seafront cafe. The fee is £112,000, a club record.

South coast rivals Southampton are my first opponents. We draw 1-1 and it's the start of four great years at the Goldstone Ground.

### May 5, 1979
### Newcastle United v. Brighton

Going for promotion after narrowly failing in my first season, we need to win at St James Park on the last day to make the top flight — and I'm out of the action, having broken my arm two weeks earlier.

The lads are magnificent and win 3-1. We're runners-up, but though there are no medals, it's the first success I've ever been involved in.

The club have hired two coaches of the Brighton Belle, tagged on to the fans' football special, to take us home. A real champagne celebration follows and we roll into Brighton station at about midnight to be greeted by 4000 supporters.

### November 17, 1979
### Nottingham Forest v. Brighton

It's hard going in the top division. I damage my ankle ligaments after five matches and the team are 22nd by the time I return. We go to Forest, who are unbeaten at home in about 30 games.

Yet we manage a 1-0 win. The game is on TV and at the end the cameras focus on me totally shattered as I'd had just one reserve comeback game before making the first team.

### February 6, 1980
### England v. Eire

My Wembley debut in a European Championship game in which two Kevin Keegan goals beat us. I still love every minute. All the Brighton lads are there to cheer me on. I'm beginning to think about a move to better myself and don't think I've done my case any harm by my performance.

### August 29, 1981
### Wolves v. Liverpool

After another struggling season at Brighton I'm anxious to leave. Suddenly Liverpool make an approach and within 20 minutes of meeting their officials, I'm Anfield-bound. I deliver my own registration forms to League HQ because I'm visiting my mother in Lytham St Annes. My first match is at Molineux.

We play them off the park and should have won by a cricket score but we end up losing 0-1. We go back to the dressing room and I'm expecting the sort of 'never mind, lads, you played well' attitude from the management I was used to at Brighton. Instead, boss Bob Paisley and his coaches give us a panning. Suddenly I realise the standards that Liverpool players have to measure up to.

### March 13, 1982
### Liverpool v. Spurs
### (Milk Cup Final)

My first major final — and I'm at fault for the eleventh minute goal by Steve Archibald that gives Spurs the lead. It stays 1-0 until three minutes from time. Then Ronnie Whelan rescues me with an equaliser. We win 3-1 after extra time. I finish the game with blood streaming from a gash on my head, but I have my first-ever medal.

### March 17, 1982
### CSKA Sofia v. Liverpool

A harsh lesson in the realities of European football as I'm sent off in Bulgaria for doing absolutely nothing.

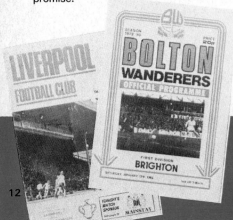

I'm hit by a late tackle and as I get to my feet, the Sofia player collapses as if he's been shot. The linesman tells the referee I hit the guy and I'm sent packing. We lose the match and we're out of the European Cup.

### May 15, 1982
### Liverpool v. Spurs

The title is clinched at Anfield — but only after we fall behind to a 35-yard Glenn Hoddle special. I score a rare 20-yarder to level and we eventually win 3-1. Two medals in my first season! I remember thinking, 'Even if I never win anything else, I'll be satisfied with those.'

### February 20, 1983
### Liverpool v. Brighton

I'm on the wrong end of a giant-killing act in the Fifth round of the FA Cup — and it's my old mates from Brighton who embarrass us. Phil Neal misses a penalty that would have given us a replay.

### March 26, 1983
### Liverpool v. Manchester United
### (Milk Cup Final)

We go behind to a Norman Whiteside goal but fight back to clinch the trophy in extra time. It has to be said, however, that injury helps us. United lose both centre-backs — Kevin Moran and Gordon McQueen — and inevitably they fade.

But it's another medal, and a second title gong comes my way as we run away with the First Division, clinching it with six games to spare.

### March 24, 1984
### Everton v. Liverpool
### (Milk Cup Final)

The Merseyside Wembley. There have been a few since, but this was the first time the clubs had met at the stadium. A brilliant atmosphere with no hint of trouble. We draw 0-0 but complete a Milk Cup hat-trick with a replay win at Maine Road.

### May 12, 1984
### Notts County v. Liverpool

Now it's a title treble. An undistinguished goalless draw at Meadow Lane does the job.

### May 30, 1984
### Roma v. Liverpool
### (European Cup Final)

We take on the Italians in their own Olympic Stadium. They are red hot favourites, but we are sharp and competitive during the weeks leading up to the game.

The atmosphere in the ground is electric. Skipper Graeme Souness makes us walk all the way round the pitch before kick-off so the home fans can give us a hot reception! It works. We're so wound up we're singing by the time we're back in the dressing-room.

I feel we always have the beating of Roma, but after 120 minutes the score is 1-1 and we face a penalty decider. Now we don't have any chance! The Anfield apprentices beat us 5-1 in a try-out penalty shoot-out just before the final.

That pessimism is borne out when Steve Nicol misses our first kick. I figure that with people such as the Brazilians Falcao and Cerezo in Roma's shooting line-up, we're on a loser.

Amazingly, Roma miss two and when Alan Kennedy blasts in the last one, the trophy is ours.

### May 29, 1985
### Juventus v. Liverpool
### (European Cup Final)

If Rome was a magnificent triumph, then Brussels was the exact opposite. The terrible tragedy which preceeded

the game will live forever in the memory of everyone who was there.

I play with a dislocated shoulder which I hoped would see me through the 90 minutes. But it goes after about three and I spend the night in the same hospital as the victims of the riot.

### May 3, 1986
### Chelsea v. Liverpool

Player-manager Kenny Dalglish scores the only goal of a victory which gives us the title. We have just pipped neighbours Everton and now we must meet them a week later in the FA Cup Final.

### May 10, 1986
### Everton v. Liverpool
### (F.A. Cup Final)

I'm sure the players of both clubs would have settled for a trophy apiece going into the season's last week. Now we can win the double.

As seems to always happen at Wembley, our opponents score first. But Ian Rush fires in a couple and Craig Johnston adds another. Kenny Dalglish's first season as boss has seen the club complete the League and Cup double for the first time in Liverpool's history.

### March 28, 1987
### Liverpool v. Wimbledon

A ruptured Achilles tendon brings my season to an end. I miss the Littlewoods Cup Final at Wembley and the battle for yet another championship. But there's a new season on the horizon and, hopefully, many more memorable matches in the offing.

# A DATE TO REMEMBER –

## Manchester United's PAUL McGRATH looks back on a turning point in his career.

⚽ December 19th, 1984, was a very significant date in both my private and professional lives. It was the day my wife Clare gave birth to our baby son, Christopher. Obviously that had an effect on my home life. How, you might well ask, did that alter my football career?

I was a Manchester United reserve team regular at that stage. Former boss Ron Atkinson was giving me occasional outings for the senior side.

I remember when Christopher arrived, ex-Old Trafford and England star Nobby Stiles congratulated me. He recalled that, when his son John, now a player for Leeds United, was born, it signalled a dramatic boost in his career.

John came into the world in May 1964. The next season Nobby established himself in the United set-up and within four years he had won three of the top trophies in football.

In 1966 he collected a World Cup winner's medal with England, and League Championship and European Cup winner's gongs for United in '67 and '68!

My son Christopher's birth didn't exactly rocket me to those dizzy heights, but, nevertheless, my career took a sudden and welcome upturn.

Ten days after Christopher's arrival, I was chosen for our away match against Chelsea. From that day on I became a fixture in the United first-team. I have missed games only through injury since. I've never been dropped!

At the end of the season, I played at Wembley in the FA Cup Final and I won my first professional medal when we beat Everton 1-0.

The following term I had a great season. Everything I did went right and I was voted runner-up to Gary Lineker in the Professional Footballers' Association Player of the Year poll. To be placed so high by fellow professionals in my first full season was a

tremendous achievement for me.

I can't ever expect to parade such a collection of famous medals that Nobby Stiles picked up in that fabulous period 20-odd years ago. However, two managers who entered my career last season can, I believe, help me towards success in the future.

On the international front it is extremely doubtful I'll ever be a World Cup winner with Eire, but Jack Charlton has certainly given the squad fresh impetus.

We have always had a squad of players who, on paper, should have been one of the best international sides in Europe. But, despite the individual quality of such as Mark Lawrenson, Liam Brady, Kevin Sheedy and Frank Stapleton, we've never put it together on the pitch. I believe Jack Charlton can alter all that.

It has been a similar story at Old Trafford. Again on paper we've possessed one of the strongest first-team pools in the country over the past few seasons.

However, despite FA Cup victories, United have been unable to blend those individual talents into a team consistent enough to win the First Division title.

If any manager can bring the championship back to Old Trafford for the first time since Nobby helped win it 20 years ago then it is Alex Ferguson. He really picked the club up by its bootlaces when he arrived from Aberdeen.

He wasn't very happy with fitness or discipline in the squad and the club generally. He and

assistant Archie Knox improved our training and made sure everybody was also neat and tidy off the field. Alex stressed the importance of representing Manchester United.

Every player whose hair was a shade on the long side had to get it cut. Club blazers replaced the colourful trendy jackets some of the lads used to wear.

I've a great respect for former boss Ron Atkinson, but he went about things in a different way to Alex Ferguson. Sure, Ron could blow his top on occasions, but it is certainly a bigger shock to the system when Alex has a go.

He launched into several real ear-bashings after some of our defeats last season. It was a case of the dressing-room door being locked on a few occasions after matches. All the rollickings he gave us were totally justified. Everything he picked up on was quite right.

To be honest we are more frightened to lose these days than we ever were. Alex Ferguson just won't stand for defeat. It is that attitude that can pave the way to success at Manchester United.

Ferguson's appointment was also the cue for me to get my game back on the right lines. Although it wasn't anything he did or said to me.

I had become a shadow of the player who had scooped second prize in the PFA awards in 1986. That had been a dream campaign for me. My form was of a very high standard throughout.

I realised it was going to be very difficult to repeat it. I had always been labelled as a cool,

14

calm defender. I was
comfortable playing my way out
of trouble in defence.

But I found I was in a panic
soon after last term kicked off.

There was a tremendous
amount of pressure on the club
to achieve something in the
season. Results didn't go well for
us early on and the critics began
to go on Ron Atkinson's back.

Nerves really gripped me.
Instead of playing the ball out of
defence, I began hoofing it
anywhere. I was just delighted to
get rid of it. I became so worried
about my game that I began to
wonder if my personal success
the previous season had been a
fluke.

Alex Ferguson took over
when Ron was sacked and it
gave me the chance to start
afresh. Ron Atkinson knew my
game well. He could see I was
having a very nervous time.

Mr. Ferguson hadn't,
however, seen a lot of me so he
couldn't make many
comparisons with my previous
form. It meant the slate was
wiped clean. Eventually my self-
belief was restored.

I realised then that I would be
capable of achieving those great
heights again. Nobby Stiles's
omen is looking good again!

15

# FLAT OUT!

Luton goalkeeper LES SEALEY stretches every muscle to bring off a fine save and thwart Everton raider ADRIAN HEATH.

CYRILLE REGIS
*Coventry City*

# An Offer I Couldn't Refuse!

## Arsenal's NIALL QUINN tells why it had to be Highbury.

⚽ When I was sixteen I decided that I wanted to be a professional sportsman . . . but the first thing I had to do was make my mind up as to which sport I wanted to make a living from!

I had the choice of three at that time — Gaelic football, Australian Rules football or soccer. And it wasn't just between three sports but three different countries as well — Ireland, Australia or England.

Gaelic football is the top team sport in Ireland and like most youngsters I started playing it at school. It's a sport in which height is very important with all the jumping and catching that's involved. Because I was always tall for my age I had a natural advantage at the game.

By the time I was fourteen, I was already playing at under-21 level and when I was sixteen, I realised that I could make a career from the game with one of the clubs in Dublin. Kevin Moran, who now plays in the centre of the defence for Manchester United, once played Gaelic football professionally and I could have done the same.

Kevin has always been known as a very brave player who takes a lot of knocks and keeps coming back. He would have got used to all that playing Gaelic football. It's a very tough sport and I would often go home from a game with blood on my legs and damaged hands. I broke several fingers playing the game, but my parents were very understanding and allowed me to keep playing.

My mother was a teacher and might have been expected to tell me to concentrate on my school work instead of playing sport. But she was never like that. I was actually quite good at school work but my mother knew that I had an excellent chance of making a career in sport, so she was quite happy to see me go training five nights a week.

I divided my time between playing Gaelic football and soccer. But I never played Rugby Union, which is another favourite sport in Ireland and I certainly didn't even consider Australian Rules football. Australian Rules, however, was obviously considering me. It is a similar game to Gaelic football so scouts were quite often over from Australian clubs to find new players.

Although I was only 16 they were very keen for me to try the game, and eventually I went to Australia for six weeks and really enjoyed it. I could have made a lot of money by staying in Australia, but I had other ideas.

I enjoyed playing Gaelic football and I'm sure Australian Rules would have been fun as well, but my great dream had always been to play soccer for Arsenal.

Football was not the number one sport in Ireland, but there was still great interest in the English game and Arsenal at that time were most people's favourites because of their three Irishmen — David O'Leary, Liam Brady and Frank Stapleton.

At first David O'Leary was my own personal hero because he played in the centre of the defence, which is where I started playing. But when I discovered that I could use my height to good effect up front, I started to watch Frank Stapleton more closely.

Since then I have always looked on Frank as the sort of player I would like to become. He has successfully combined power in the air with skill on the ground and that is what I'm working towards.

So when I was given the chance to go to London to sign on with Arsenal I forgot all about Gaelic and Australian Rules football. I was taking a big risk at the time but I know now that I made the right decision.

In fact I've been very lucky so far in my career at Highbury because everything seems to have happened so quickly. I hadn't been in the reserves for very long when I was given my

overdo it with the heavy stuff.

Last season was a learning process for me and I relished the experience of playing in the number nine shirt that Frank Stapleton had worn along with so many other fine players at Highbury. It was a great honour for me and I was determined to make the most of it.

In many ways I was surprised to be playing at all last season. When George Graham became manager he would have looked at the scoring charts and seen that I'd scored only one goal in my first dozen games in the side and that was in my debut game against Liverpool. I thought I would have to wait for my turn but the manager gave me a chance and I did my best to take it.

For nearly the whole of my first season there was talk of Arsenal buying another striker and at first this worried me a lot. After a while though I realised that I was playing quite well and that I could give anybody a good fight for that treasured number nine shirt. I didn't want to let it go if I could help it.

Everything that happened last season was quite incredible for me. We did very well in the league, we won at Wembley in the Littlewoods Cup Final and I was also picked to play for my country.

When I was making the decision about which sport to make my profession, I would never have guessed how quickly everything would work out for me. If I had chosen Gaelic or Australian Rules football and not soccer I would have been stuck in one country and been known only there. Soccer gives me the opportunity to do so much more.

Now I just have to keep improving all the time. It took a while for the rest of the team to realise that I could play a bit and that I didn't always have to have the ball high in the air. I'm just as happy with the ball at my feet.

Like a lot of the present Arsenal team I'm still young and have a lot to prove. But by the time I finish my career at Highbury I hope that I will be remembered as a great player — just like Frank Stapleton.

chance in the first team.

There couldn't have been a better time to make my debut because Liverpool were the visitors to Highbury and I was called in to play up front alongside Charlie Nicholas. And it turned out to be a dream start as Charlie and I scored the goals in our 2-0 win.

It was a moment I shall never forget. I was very lucky to be playing with someone like Charlie Nicholas, who was a great help to me in my first year in the team. There were times when Charlie was going through a bad patch himself but he still managed to encourage me and get me through a game.

It is a very tough job playing as a centre-forward in the First Division and you need to be very strong to play in that position, so I've had to work hard on building myself up. Everybody was calling me "Beanpole Quinn" when I first got in the team, but I'm much stronger now.

Last season was my first full term in the team and for much of it I felt very tired towards the end of matches. But gradually I started to last the ninety minutes much better. Weight training was a big help — although I didn't

NIGEL CLOUGH
Nottingham Forest

**BRIAN MARWOOD**
*Sheffield Wednesday*

21

# When Tough Guys Tangle

There was no holding back in this challenge between Wimbledon's stop-at-nothing striker JOHN FASHANU and Spurs' tough-tackling GARY MABBUTT! Amazingly, both players survived unscathed!

**RUSSELL OSMAN**
*Leicester City*

23

# HAVE BOOTS- WILL TRAVEL!

## That's the go-anywhere approach of Charlton's Happy Wanderer JIM MELROSE

⚽ I've always liked to think of myself as a striker with a nose for goals. But it's been my nose that has caused me a lot of problems in my career!

Ever since I was a young lad in Scotland I've suffered from hay fever — which isn't too good for a boy who wanted to become a footballer.

But I wasn't going to let that stop me and although at times I've finished up with streaming eyes after a match, it hasn't prevented me playing. Maybe it's a good thing that we don't play much football in the summer when the pollen count is high, and people like me really suffer!

The problem has got worse over the last few seasons because I've broken my nose on several occasions. As a striker you have to take risks and that inevitably means I've picked up a few knocks — and that includes plenty of facial injuries.

I've scored a few goals by going in where it hurts and this style has usually made me popular with the fans at all the different clubs I've been with.

24

It has been the story of my career so far that I've moved around a lot from one club to another. I've been lucky that I'm a striker and teams always need somebody who can score goals.

To be honest, I think I would have scored a lot more goals if I'd played for slightly better teams, but I've often been at clubs struggling to avoid relegation.

It all started for me at Partick Thistle in Scotland, where I was a part-timer but still managed to win 8 caps for Scotland at Under-21 level. The next stop after Partick was Leicester City, which proved to be one of my favourite clubs.

While I was at Filbert Street I enjoyed a particularly good

**LENNIE LAWRENCE —**
limited choice at Charlton.

relationship with the fans and probably the best season there was when I played up-front with Gary Lineker.

At that stage Gary was quite young but he had plenty of pace and a good eye for goal. I can't say that I knew he would become a great star but I thought he had the potential. Gary has certainly managed to make the most of that potential!

Gary and I played about 40 games together in the first team and scored a lot of goals, but unfortunately I had to move on before the partnership had a chance to develop further.

The next port of call took me back to Glasgow to play for Celtic. For a lot of players that would have been a dream move, and it was certainly the biggest club I've played for. Unfortunately, though, it didn't work out for me.

I was used to having the fans on my side but that just wasn't the case at Celtic even though I still scored goals there. The problem was I had always been a Rangers fan and the Celtic supporters knew that only too well and wouldn't let me forget it.

While I was at Celtic I did play in a Scottish League Cup Final and a Scottish Cup Final, coming on twice as substitute. Alas, we lost on both occasions. But after that it was time to move on again after only 29 League games for the club.

I had a short spell on loan to Wolves but the next major move took me to Manchester City. In my first season at Maine Road I managed to help the club win promotion back to Division 1. Having started the season with Wolves, who struggled from the start and were to finish up bottom of the division, I found myself playing for a much better City side.

That season at City was rather typical of my career because there was a spell in the middle of it when I scored a lot of goals and helped City climb right into the promotion picture. No striker can keep going all the time and unfortunately I had a very barren period in the second half of that season.

Although we were promoted that term, nobody got very many goals. I did manage to score though when it came to the crucial last game of the season when we needed to beat Charlton, who were to be my next club, in the match at Maine Road. We won 5-1 that day to go up with a touch of style at the expense of Portsmouth.

So I was back in the First Division again but unfortunately it wasn't to be a great return for me. I couldn't hold down a regular first team place and eventually I moved on again.

It was just before the transfer deadline in March 1986 that I signed for Charlton and again I found myself with the challenge of helping another team reach the First Division. When I arrived at the club there were just 11 games to go and they were just out of the promotion places.

There was no real time to settle in — they needed goals straight away and thankfully I managed to score five which helped Charlton to finish second and take them into the top flight for the first time in 29 years.

We always knew it would be very hard for us in the First Division. The top clubs all have big squads to choose from but our manager Lennie Lawrence had a much smaller staff at his disposal. There were some players with First Division experience but we also had a lot of young players playing at that level for the first time. It was always going to be difficult and we relied heavily on the great team spirit that exists between the players.

But despite the fact that it was a very hard season, there were a few highlights and my special memory is the hat-trick I scored against Everton. It was the first time I'd scored three goals in a game for Charlton, and to score them against a top side like Everton made it even better.

They have international-class players throughout their side and I was up against two of them that day in central defenders Kevin Ratcliffe and Dave Watson. To penetrate that barrier three times was quite an achievement.

Another highlight last season was to play at Wembley in the Full-Members Cup final although in the end we lost to Blackburn.

Not too many players get the chance to play at Wembley in their career so I was just happy to go there — whatever the match or the result. I'm just hoping now that I'll have a few more big occasions to look forward to during my career, whoever I might find myself playing for.

# Just The Job, Joe

A high cross into the Celtic goalmouth — a bullet header by Aberdeen striker JOE MILLER — that's the recipe for a spectacular goal in a clash between two of Scotland's top teams.

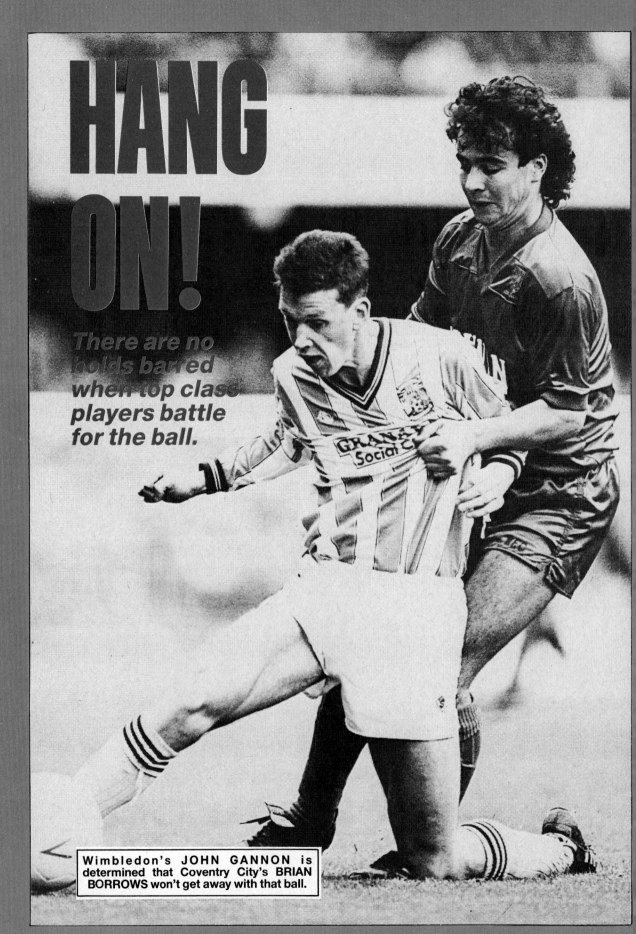

# HANG ON!

*There are no holds barred when top class players battle for the ball.*

Wimbledon's JOHN GANNON is determined that Coventry City's BRIAN BORROWS won't get away with that ball.

Aston Villa's GARRY THOMPSON can't escape the close attentions of ROBERT ISAAC (Chelsea).

Wimbledon's DENNIS WISE finds he can't escape from the GLENN HODDLE hold.

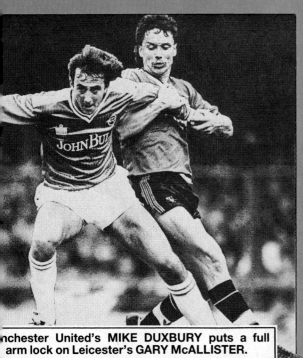

anchester United's MIKE DUXBURY puts a full arm lock on Leicester's GARY McALLISTER.

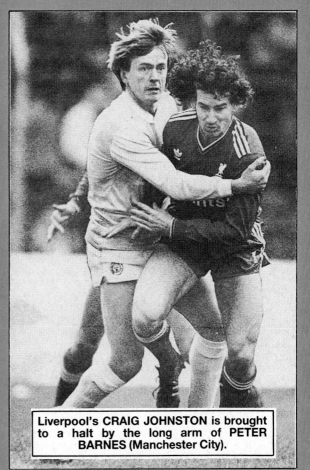

Liverpool's CRAIG JOHNSTON is brought to a halt by the long arm of PETER BARNES (Manchester City).

# Get 'Em Involved!

## That's the driving force behind a campaign to take football to the fans.

⚽ The dressing-room is buzzing. It's Cup Final day, and Alex Ferguson and Archie Knox have just completed their last-minute pep-talk. The Manchester United players can't wait to get on to the pitch and start the action.

Later, in the same dressing-room, the atmosphere bubbles with excitement. The match has been won, and United have secured their first trophy under Ferguson's managership.

The recurring dream of an avid United fan? Not one bit of it. The scenario just described actually happened last season — just five weeks to be exact after Fergie's appointment as Manchester United's manager.

What's more, victory was achieved without stars like Bryan Robson, Gordon Strachan, Norman Whiteside and Paul McGrath.

The team consisted of a group of local unemployed youths, and the tournament was the curtain-raiser to last season's Guinness soccer sixes at Manchester's G-MEX centre.

The involvement of Manchester United — plus five other North-West clubs, is just one example of how the senior football outfits have been trying to help the community at large.

Last season, the Professional Footballers' Association got together with the Football League to launch a new scheme called "The Community Programme in Professional Football."

Funded by the Manpower Services Commission, the aim is to forge closer links between the clubs and the general public.

United, along with Manchester City, Oldham Athletic, Bolton Wanderers, Bury and Preston North End, were chosen to operate a pilot scheme.

It has been so successful the organisers plan to spread the programme throughout the country, with all 92 League clubs becoming involved.

At each participating club, a

ENTHUSIASTS — Manchester United's management duo, Alex Ferguson (left) and Archie Knox.

former player is employed full-time, and, helped by several assistants, he arranges events in the area.

Among other activities, they visit schools to coach the youngsters, supervise training sessions and tournaments for the local unemployed, and organise sports evenings for the general public at various centres.

The man leading Manchester United's contribution is their former European Cup medal winner and England internationalist, Brian Kidd.

Says Brian, "The most important part of our work is helping school kids.

"We invite the schools in the area to write to us and arrange a series of visits. When we arrive, we're quite prepared to either take the sessions over completely, or simply assist the school's sports master.

"We do insist, however, that the boys with lesser ability get as much attention as the more skilful players.

"We wouldn't be interested in going to schools which simply wanted a bit of coaching for their established football team.

"Our school visits have become so popular that we are now booked up for months in advance," Brian goes on.

"But one of the most pleasing results is the way in which we've helped the development of youngsters who are not so naturally gifted.

"Alex Ferguson and club chairman Martin Edwards have each received a number of letters from grateful schoolmasters explaining that several boys, who'd previously sat out PE classes and sporting activities, have now gone through the full range of sports and are competing for places in their school teams.

"As an extension of our school coaching sessions, we have now fixed a regular Wednesday night match at The Cliff (Manchester United's training ground), when we invite two of the schools we have visited recently to play against each other.

"Even those games have had a spin-off. The sports masters

themselves have been so keen to take part that we have been setting up a series of matches between the teachers and United's backroom staff.

"The idea has been such a hit within the club that Alex Ferguson and his assistant, Archie Knox, are making sure that theirs are the first names to be put on the team sheet!

"Alex, in particular, has been very enthusiastic about every aspect of the programme.

"When we held an impromptu six-a-side tournament at a local sports centre, 89 teams entered and Alex was only too pleased to present trophies to the Under-16 and Under-13 winners on the Old Trafford pitch before last season's home match against Arsenal.

"In fact, the whole United staff were extremely helpful in giving the lads a smashing day out at the stadium as part of their winners' prize.

"Alex has also encouraged the United first team players to make appearances at our schools to give talks or briefly join in the coaching sessions whenever their own training schedules allow.

"Paul McGrath was one of the first to attend, while Graeme Hogg and Remi Moses have gone out of their way to present prizes on our competition days.

"The United boss has also supported our involvement with local unemployed people. We've set up a League for them, and the six participating clubs were also invited to enter two six-a-side teams for the curtain-raiser to the Guinness tournament.

"Alex and Archie were only too pleased to give our lads their pre-match pep-talk. That boosted them no end, and must have helped them win the trophy."

Now that Brian and his helpers have established their network in the local football community, they have been able to branch out and offer help to the Manchester public who are interested in other sports.

"The supervisors at the other clubs have also come up with their own thoughts on how to involve more local people, so we

KEEN TO LEND A HAND —
**Paul McGrath
(Manchester United).**

meet regularly to exchange ideas," Brian points out.

"There are also weekly meetings with Mick Burns, the PFA's education officer, and Roger Reade, the scheme's chief administrator, who are monitoring our progress.

"The original reason for the scheme, which was the brainchild of the PFA, was to give something back to the community.

"The PFA, concerned that football had been getting a lot of bad publicity, were also worried that the fans were being taken too much for granted.

"After the first year of the scheme, I'm sure that the organisers and the fans we've been able to help will agree that it has been a big success so far."

**ALLAN EVANS**
*Aston Villa*

**GORDON DURIE**
*Chelsea*

33

# It's Changed Days

## Coventry City's TREVOR PEAKE explains why.

⚽ Team spirit and professionalism. These are the two words that would spring to mind if I was asked to sum up the 'new' Coventry City.

Last season saw a major breakthrough for the club. After years of struggling to survive in the First Division, we not only finished well up the table, but we also won the FA Cup for the first time in the club's history.

And it can all be put down to a complete change in attitude that spread through Highfield Road after George Curtis, the managing director, and team boss John Sillett took over the reins.

They put together a strong squad, gave the team 'play football' instructions, and worked on developing a strong bond between the players.

We had had little continuity of any kind during my time at Highfield Road. In my first three and a half years at the club I lined up with 51 different players.

Even now, although I've completed only four seasons and have well under 200 League games behind me, I've played more matches for City than any other player currently at the club.

We have got to know our colleagues at last. There was a time when you wondered who you would be changing next to at training each morning.

Players would come and go with great regularity. Most would play only a few games before they were on their way again. That type of thing doesn't lend itself to creating the attitude necessary to become a successful side.

You couldn't, for instance, hope to strike up an understanding with your immediate partner on the field. Until Brian Kilcline became a regular with me in defence, I'd played alongside half a dozen centre-halves in less than two seasons.

But now the squad is much more stable, and the teamwork which stems from that makes it so much more difficult for opponents.

To illustrate that spirit, I'll tell you about the day we played Sheffield Wednesday at Hillsborough in the quarter-finals of the FA Cup last season.

We had already won two extremely difficult away ties at Manchester United and Stoke and the confidence when we travelled to Sheffield was sky-high.

We were in the dressing-room prior to the kick-off. John Sillett had finished his pep talk. There were a couple of minutes to fill before we were called on to the pitch.

Suddenly, John started to sing. Then all the lads joined in. When the signal came for us to make our way to the tunnel, all you could hear was the chant — usually reserved for the fans — 'Here we go, here we go, here we go.'

At half-time we did it again. The Wednesday players must have heard us. I don't know if it affected them or not, but we won the match 3-1.

I have never witnessed

34

# At Highfield Road

anything like it. Players are normally very reluctant to behave like that. But it just showed the self-belief which grew within the club last season.

Much of the credit for the changes at Coventry must go to the management. They have, without question, made us a much more professional outfit.

We were told at the start of the season, for example, that we must wear club blazers, slacks and ties at all matches. Not only would we look smart, we would also be showing we had pride in the club we play for.

The players were taken away to a hotel during the week prior to cup-ties to enable us to prepare for the match properly.

We were also offered hotel accommodation if young babies or sick children threatened to disturb a good night's sleep before games. We were taken for team dinners ... golfing trips were arranged for us.

And, for our part, the players set up a committee which organises social functions such as discos and dinner dances, but which also deals with indiscipline within the club.

We drew up a strict schedule of fines — all based on a percentage of a player's wage, so that younger lads and apprentices are hit in proportion to the senior men.

There are fines for on-field indiscipline, plus penalties for being late for training or team bus, forgetting your club tie, even for being late handing in your voting slip nominating the worst player in training every day!

I'm on the committee, along with the other senior players at the club — goalkeeper Steve Ogrizovic, captain Brian Kilcline, striker Cyrille Regis and left-back Greg Downs.

But there was a time when it seemed fairly unlikely I'd ever achieve the status of 'senior player' at Coventry. After I joined

the club from Lincoln City in the summer of 1983, I had a very difficult time settling into the club.

I arrived along with several other players from the lower divisions. We had been bought by the then manager Bobby Gould to replace established stars who had left the club.

City had lost Gary Gillespie to Liverpool, Mark Hateley to Portsmouth, Danny Thomas to Tottenham, Steve Whitton to West Ham, Gary Thompson to West Brom and Paul Dyson to Stoke. The new batch included Micky Adams from Gillingham, Micky Gynn from Peterborough, Dave Bennett (Cardiff), Dave Bamber (Blackpool) and Nicky Platnauer and Graham Withey from Bristol Rovers.

I certainly had a lot of problems adapting initially to the higher standard of football and wondered at times if I might have been better joining Second Division Huddersfield Town instead. They had tried to buy me from Lincoln that summer.

My form was poor and even though I was being picked every week, I was concerned enough to pay a couple of visits to Bobby Gould's office to tell him I wasn't happy.

I had the impression, too, that

some of the established men resented the newcomers because of their backgrounds. They felt we were a bit beneath them as we had played most of our football outside the top level.

It didn't make settling any easier — nor did the fact that I felt I needed to succeed at Coventry because the move from Lincoln was very much a 'homecoming' for me. Most of my family live in the area and I played with Nuneaton Borough — just up the road from Coventry — before I signed for Lincoln.

But after about three months at Highfield Road, I managed to have what I'd describe as my first decent match for the club and, despite that difficult opening, I still managed to win an extra year on top of my initial two-year contract at the end of my first season. Since then I've felt much more comfortable in the First Division.

I got my first sniff of real success very late in my career — I was 30 when I played in the Cup Final — but you know what they say about better late than not at all.

I just hope the next seasons at Coventry continue the good work achieved last term. Then perhaps there will be more exciting things ahead.

**THE TEAM BEHIND THE COVENTRY REVIVAL — Managing director George Curtis (left) and team coach John Sillett.**

# AWAY FROM THE ROAR OF THE CROWD...

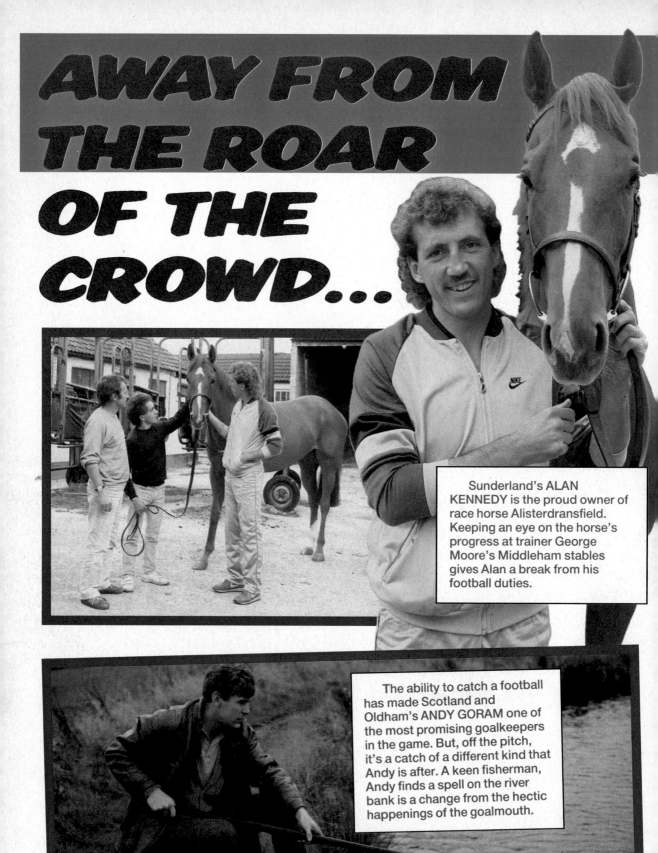

Sunderland's ALAN KENNEDY is the proud owner of race horse Alisterdransfield. Keeping an eye on the horse's progress at trainer George Moore's Middleham stables gives Alan a break from his football duties.

The ability to catch a football has made Scotland and Oldham's ANDY GORAM one of the most promising goalkeepers in the game. But, off the pitch, it's a catch of a different kind that Andy is after. A keen fisherman, Andy finds a spell on the river bank is a change from the hectic happenings of the goalmouth.

Players who face the pressures of top flight football need to find time to unwind and relax. Here's how four top performers get away from it all.

When JEFF CLARKE (ex-Newcastle) takes a break from football, he spends his time growing vegetables. And judging by these prize-winning cabbages, it seems that there's a touch of "greenfingers" about the big defender.

At his smallholding in the country with his chickens, ducks and dogs, Fulham's GORDON DAVIES finds the atmosphere makes a welcome break from the ups and downs of football.

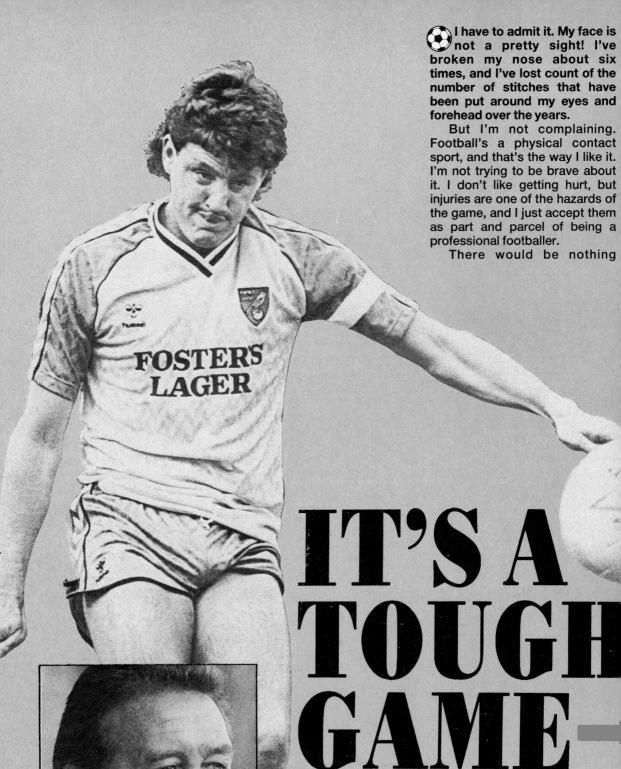

I have to admit it. My face is not a pretty sight! I've broken my nose about six times, and I've lost count of the number of stitches that have been put around my eyes and forehead over the years.

But I'm not complaining. Football's a physical contact sport, and that's the way I like it. I'm not trying to be brave about it. I don't like getting hurt, but injuries are one of the hazards of the game, and I just accept them as part and parcel of being a professional footballer.

There would be nothing

# IT'S A TOUGH GAME

and that's the way I like it
says Norwich City's
STEVE BRUCE

▲ *KEN BROWN* — he keeps the record straight.

worse in my book than trying to make football a non-contact sport. The fans love the physical challenges — as long as they are fairly given and taken.

The best games are the ones that are hard fought with players getting stuck in. Skill will still tell in the end if every player gives one hundred per cent.

My favourite players are the strikers who give and take knocks without complaint. Men like Mick Harford of Luton, and ex-Aston Villa and England Peter Withe, now with Sheffield United. They can give and take a bashing out on the pitch, do it fairly, without moaning at the knocks — and then join you for a chat after the game.

I don't condone rough play or dirty tactics. There's no place in the game for over-the-top lunges that can break a player's leg. But for me the game wouldn't be the same without the physical challenges, and playing in the centre of defence you are almost bound to pick up some injuries.

I've broken my nose so often it's not worth having it re-set until I pack up playing. When I hang up my boots I'll go into hospital for an operation to rebuild my nose — if they can find the pieces! When I come out of hospital my wife won't know me! Until then I'll put up with my 'lived-in' look and go on enjoying a hard game.

Last season, in the space of a couple of weeks, I played virtually a full game with a broken nose and another with a cracked bone in my leg. I didn't come off because I was enjoying the games. Injuries are bound to happen. I just try to ignore them.

I love playing football. I'd be the same if I was an amateur, playing the game for nothing. Money doesn't come into it. But I must admit that right through my career there has often been an extra motivation for me.

When I was with Gillingham, and since I've been at Norwich, there always seems to have been transfer speculation involving my name.

Whether there was anything in it or not, the effect on me has always been the same. I've gone out for the next game thinking 'Well, if so-and-so is watching me, I'm going to do my best to impress him'.

In the past couple of years some of the biggest clubs in Britain have been linked with me, and it's very flattering. Teams like Everton, Manchester United, Spurs, Arsenal and Newcastle have all been mentioned as 'interested' in me.

It always turns your head a bit when you read your name being linked with clubs like that. It was the same — in a lesser way, of course — when I was at Gillingham. There was always said to be clubs interested in signing me.

At Gillingham the prospect of being given the chance to play in a higher division was a tremendous incentive. On a cold, wet afternoon at the likes of Scunthorpe or Rotherham, that extra motivation was always a big help in producing my very best.

Of course, you never know if the rumours are true. In those situations the player is usually the last to hear about it. Certainly at Gillingham I was never told if clubs had made a bid — and I've since discovered that a few did. In the end Norwich signed me — but only after I'd let my contract run out, and turned down a new one.

There has been even more speculation since I established myself in the City side, but at least manager Ken Brown puts me in the picture. If there's been a transfer story about me in the Press, he'll take me aside at training and tell me the strength of the story.

He's always said that if someone did make a genuine offer, I would be among the first to know — I wouldn't read it in the Press first. But it's still a bit unsettling for my wife and family to read transfer stories. The phone never stops ringing with people asking what's happening.

The truth is I'm happy to be playing for Norwich. It's a very friendly club, but one with ambition. If I were to leave, there are not many clubs in Britain I could go to and better myself.

Dave Watson won the first of his England caps while a Norwich player, and I'd like to think I could follow him into the international squad. I haven't given up hope of winning a call-up from Bobby Robson — even if the nearest I've come so far to international football is with Northern Ireland!

My mother comes from Northern Ireland, and last year I got a call from Belfast asking if I'd be interested in playing for the Irish side in the Mexico World Cup. The only problem was that I'd already played for the England Youth team while at Gillingham, and that youth cap commits me to playing only for England.

I'm not unhappy about that. I'm very much an Englishman. I shall plug away just hoping to attract Bobby Robson's attention at some stage.

Norwich are not the 'country bumpkins' they were once made out to be. The club is as well organised and go-ahead as any of the big city outfits.

The superb new stand at Carrow Road is a good example. When the club's main stand was burnt down a couple of years ago it could have been a disaster for Norwich. Instead, the club hasn't looked back, establishing a place among the leading group in the First Division last season.

I will never forget the time the stand burned down because although it was very sad at the time, it provided me with one of my funniest moments in the game.

The day after the fire the players were all in the changing room at the training ground discussing the disaster and feeling a bit 'down'. Suddenly the door burst open, and striker John Deehan charged in — wearing a fireman's uniform and helmet!

"Where's the fire?" he was shouting, and all the lads just burst out laughing.

John's next door neighbour was a fireman, and John had borrowed his gear as a practical joke.

It certainly raised our spirits, and after that we never let the situation get us down — even while we had to use the pub next to the ground as a dressing-room.

We fought back from the effects of the fire. We bounced back from relegation to the Second Division, and now I feel we have helped to put Norwich on the football map.

I've had three great years at Carrow Road. I have especially enjoyed the responsibility of skippering the team for the last year.

I've been proud to lead out a side that has established a place in the top half of the First Division. It has made all the knocks worthwhile.

NEIL McNAB
*Manchester City*

ALAN DEVONSHIRE
West Ham United

41

# HARD WORK –

## That's the recipe for success of Derby County manager ARTHUR COX

⚽ In guiding Derby County back to the First Division last season, manager Arthur Cox was repeating his achievement of three years before with his previous club, Newcastle United.

But, on that occasion, Cox left his players to do their celebrating, packed his bags and left St James' Park to take up the challenge offered at the Baseball Ground.

In many ways, the job posed a much stiffer test. For starters, Derby had plummeted to the Third Division after their glory days, when they won two League Championships in the 1970's.

Cox set about resurrecting the club with his usual style — hard work and a minimum of fuss. With his close-cropped hairstyle and clipped tones, he carries the air of a regimental sergeant-major. His approach to management, and the demands he makes on his players, befits such an image.

Playing for Derby is all about discipline and not expecting too much praise for doing your job properly.

When Derby went top of the Second Division by beating Blackburn Rovers 3-2 last season, the players' celebrations were cut dead the moment they entered the dressing-room at full time.

Cox was furious that they'd allowed Rovers back into the match with two second half goals. Even striker Bobby Davison, who'd scored a brace, didn't escape a rollicking.

But nobody can accuse Cox of not living up to the standards he sets for others. He lives, eats and sleeps football, and no amount of hard work is too much for him.

He says, "I love every minute of it. Can't get to the ground quickly enough every day. Football is a marvellous game. It's there to be enjoyed and I just love it.

"Taking a day off, for example, comes hard. I'd rather watch a game at any level, then go home and watch more on video. Perhaps because I make that kind of demand on myself, I make similar demands on my players.

"I'm hard with them. In fact, if there's a harder taskmaster in the game, I don't think I would like to meet him. I don't go in for lots of praise. When a player does well, he is merely doing the job he is paid to do. I don't believe in patting him on the back and saying 'Well done.'"

That philosophy is one which County defender Ross MacLaren experienced as soon as he arrived at the club two years ago.

Cox had no sooner signed the former Shrewsbury Town skipper than he gave him a real dressing-down with the accusation, "You can't defend, can't head a ball and you have no pace."

If that blast was designed to bring the best out of the new signing, then the strategy had an immediate effect. For the next few months, MacLaren dominated the man-of-the-match awards as Derby embarked on the run which was to result in two promotions in consecutive years.

Says Ross, "The boss gave my ego a bit of a dent, but he also brought about an immediate improvement in my game. His first demand was that I lose half a stone from my normal playing weight. I did that, and felt the benefit right away.

"He also made me a much more disciplined player, which has helped me to stay out of trouble with referees. I used to lose the rag easily and was often booked. Not any more. Thanks to the boss, I no longer have a hot-headed nature.

"And I know that, should I ever let my standards slip, he'd be the first to pull me back into line."

Perhaps it's the constant search for improvement that makes Cox loathe to dish out bouquets, while he's never slow to react to failure.

While manager of Newcastle United, his players knew they were in for a rocket after losing a Milk Cup-tie at Oxford — and Cox didn't fail them.

He recalls, "The dressing-room wasn't a pretty sight afterwards. The doors were locked for so long, we ended up having fish and chips brought in while harsh words were exchanged.

"Three days later, we produced our best performance of the season, beating Manchester City 5-0. But that wasn't achieved on the training field. It began while eating those fish and chips."

Cox's sergeant-major reputation goes back to his days as a coach with Preston North End, and in particular his eve-of-match routine.

He'd take the players outside the ground to an area behind one of the Deepdale stands and order them to run on the spot — on tip-toes!

After starting at a slow pace, he'd shout "Go" midway through the routine, at which point the players were expected to go flat-out.

The reason for taking them to that particular spot was because the acoustics beneath the stand were such that he could hear the echo of their footsteps if they were working hard enough! Failure to detect those sound waves meant the players had to start all over again.

# AND NO FUSS!

Cox is a great believer in the theory that, if you lead your life well and develop the right habits, then you have a better chance of doing your job properly.

That was a doctrine he passed on to former Newcastle star John Bird, when the latter was a young player at Preston.

John reveals, "Arthur Cox was the biggest influence on my career. He taught me the right things to do.

"I recall a little shop across the road from Deepdale, where the players used to buy pasties and cola after training.

"This was frowned upon by Arthur Cox, who considered such a diet was not suitable for footballers. He made it clear that anyone seen consuming those items in future would have to face his wrath.

"Consequently, we developed a black-market trade in pasties and cola. The lady in the shop would put a batch aside for us. We'd go round to the back door of the premises to buy them, then sit on the wall outside to eat them.

"One day I went into the shop and forgot the rules. I came out the front door with a pastie in one hand and a can of cola in the other.

"At the same moment, Arthur Cox emerged from the main door of Deepdale, glanced up and sprinted across the road towards me. He then delivered a flying kick which sent the pastie and cola spinning from my hands and into the road. It was a lesson I never forgot."

It's no coincidence that most of the complimentary remarks made about Cox are from players who have served under him. The last person you'll hear praising Arthur Cox is the man himself.

If there's one thing he shies away from, it's personal image-building.

That's probably reflected in the fact that armchair fans have never seen him airing his views on TV football panels or seeking the glare of the spotlight.

He admits, "I hate it when people in the game — managers, coaches and players — try to glorify themselves. My strength is working with players, and I believe that football managers in the main should be more seen than heard.

"The public aren't really interested in what I have to say. They are more interested in what I do behind the scenes to help give them a team to be proud of.

"The lads who sweat blood and tears for 90 minutes are the people fans want to equate with — not the manager.

"My job, and that of the players, is to send those fans home happy, and I prefer to let my players do what talking needs to be done."

That attitude is one he shared with one of his sporting idols — the late Bill Shankly.

On the first day of his managership at Newcastle, Cox received a telephone call from the former Liverpool boss.

Shanks told him, "Listen, son. Don't worry about the directors, worry about the supporters. And if you give them a successful Newcastle team, there won't be a piece of granite big enough in Aberdeen to build you a throne."

Maybe that hunk of stone still doesn't exist. But if Cox continues his run of success at the Baseball Ground, the County fans will surely be happy to give him the freedom of Derby instead.

**JOHN FASHANU**
*Wimbledon*

# THE JUNK FOOD KID -

⚽ Saturday August 17, 1985, is a date which will always be etched in my memory. It was the opening day of the new season and I was making my First Division debut for Newcastle United at Southampton.

Pulling on the black and white first team jersey for the very first time was the realisation of a dream I'd had since joining the club as a 13-year-old, five years earlier.

But what made the moment all the sweeter was that it came barely weeks after a period when my main worry was that I might be shown the door at St. James' Park.

I'd never had any doubts about my ability as a midfield player. Nor, I believe, had anyone at the club who had worked with me since I was a schoolboy.

But, early in the summer of '85, Jack Charlton, then the Newcastle manager, pulled me aside one day and delivered a short, sharp message that rocked me back on my heels.

I was coming towards the end of my apprenticeship and, despite having just helped the club lift the F.A. Youth Cup, I knew the previous term had been something of a nightmare for me.

Big Jack's "words of wisdom" merely reflected that.

"I'm not sure about you, son," he told me. "I'm going to give you another few weeks before deciding your future. It's up to you."

The boss's words stung me, no doubt about that, but neither did I have doubts about the reasons behind his indecision.

Frankly, my attitude to the game in the previous season hadn't been all it might have been. I was also having problems keeping my weight down because of some pretty silly eating habits.

That, in fact, was the major source of my troubles. I'd even earned the unenviable reputation as the "junk-food" kid within the club . . . and deservedly so.

Sweets, chocolates, Chinese take-aways. You name it, I'd eat it. Worst of all, I was a compulsive nibbler.

Looking back, I now realise I was doing myself no favours. In fact, if I'd continued in the same vein I might even have been in danger of putting my career in jeopardy.

## t was the label d to live down s PAUL GASCOIGNE WCASTLE UNITED)

I'd be the first to admit that but for coaches Willie McFaul (now manager) and Colin Suggett I might already have eaten my way out of St James' Park.

Willie and Colin had spent a lot of time with me the previous season. Not the least because they clearly realised I had a problem when it came to food.

I'll always be grateful that they made the effort to help me by sorting out my diet.

Every day after training they'd whisk me off to a local restaurant and make sure I ate the type of meal needed.

They insisted I tuck into a good steak or fresh salad and ignore all the stodge I'd previously been devouring. Colin was forever handing me diet sheets.

The outcome was that I did start to lose weight. Not only that, I began to look and feel better. Much more like a well-conditioned footballer.

Clearly, however, Jack Charlton still remained unconvinced that I'd totally mastered my eating habits and my attitude to the game. Hence his warning. I've got to thank Jack for reminding me what was at stake if I didn't look after myself.

What it also meant was I didn't even think about taking a "break" for the remainder of that close-season. I doubt if I've ever worked harder, voluntarily at that, to try to prove myself.

I trained on my own throughout the summer months. I was even out pounding the roads at midnight on occasions.

Fortunately, that late-late-training-show did wonders for me. I shed pounds in weight. But the real reward came on the opening day of that 1985-86 season when I was handed my first-team chance.

Jack Charlton had departed on the eve of the campaign, but his successor, Willie McFaul, showed his faith in my ability by plunging me somewhat unexpectedly into the First Division firing line.

It was the stuff of which dreams are made. And really that's the way my first taste of the big-time action continued for most of that season.

It was something special paying first-time visits to places like Anfield and Old Trafford. And the nine League goals I managed to grab put the seal on it all.

Last term, of course, didn't turn out quite so well. I spent a large part of the campaign, something like five months, on the sidelines through injury.

But none of that has dented my ambition to get to the very top of the footballing tree. I can unashamedly admit that I don't want to just make a living from the game. I want just as much to earn a reputation as a really high-class performer.

I know it will take time and dedication. But I've already set

my sights as high as possible. My dream is to one day play at full international level for England.

That ambition, in fact, has been fuelled even more since my team-mate Peter Beardsley made it big on the England scene.

It was marvellous listening to Peter after he came back from the Mexico World Cup Finals in '86. He had a wealth of stories to tell. But not the least was the immense pride he showed that goes with pulling on an England jersey.

It's those kind of emotions I want to sample as a player in future. And I'm determined that I won't fail to make the grade for the want of trying.

I've probably got to accept that I'll always have a battle with the scales. I simply seem the type who can put on weight just looking at food.

But, unlike days of old, I think I've learned how to keep a potential problem under control. Just as I like to think my attitude to the game is now on the right wavelength.

It calls for dedication to attain the heights I've set myself . . . and I'm not about to let myself down. Nor the many people who have helped my career over the past two or three years!

PETER BEARDSLEY

JOHN McCLELLAND
*Watford*

umbro

48

**PETER REID**
*Everton*

49

# THAT JERSEY

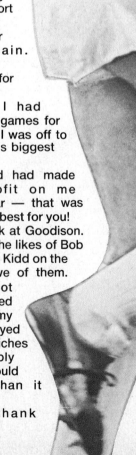

⚽ My career, crammed with transfers, managers, striking partners and clubs, has the look of that of a veteran spanning almost two decades and close on 1000 games.

Yet, I am only 28, have been on the circuit for a mere nine seasons and have clocked up barely 250 League matches.

However, my file reads thus: six clubs; nine managers; one million pounds worth of transfer deals; and a list of 24 different striking partners.

My career began with Tottenham Hotspur where I spent three months as a junior but was then released.

I went into non-League football with Letchworth and supplemented my wages by working as an asphalt roofer for a mate's dad.

I also popped in regularly to my local club Luton Town and I trained at Kenilworth Road. It was there I met the biggest influence on my career — the late Harry Haslam.

I never actually signed for Luton and didn't really think much of it when Harry was lured up to Yorkshire to manage Sheffield United. I was just sad that I wouldn't have him around to help me any more.

Within days of Harry taking over at Bramall Lane, I received a surprise telephone call from him. His message was pretty simple, "If you want to sign for United, jump on a train to Sheffield!" With that I made a late and surprising entry into professional football.

Harry Haslam's strength was his ability to wheel and deal in the transfer market.

He almost pulled off the coup of getting Argentinian World Cup aces Ossie Ardiles and Ricky Villa to Sheffield in '82.

The club, unfortunately, couldn't afford them and in the end Harry was instrumental in the World Cup stars going to Tottenham.

That jaunt across the world shows Harry's brilliance in transfers. As I said, I had been involved in one of his deals when he snapped me up for United. I didn't realise I was going to be involved in another one so quickly.

Eleven months after I joined the Second Division outfit, Sheffield United's chairman told Harry that he wanted some money raised before the transfer deadline.

That gave Harry just five days to sort something out. But his wheeler-dealer magic worked again. He arranged a £100,000 transfer for me to Everton! I was stunned. I had played just six full games for the Blades and yet I was off to one of the country's biggest outfits.

Sheffield United had made a £100,000 profit on me in less than a year — that was Harry Haslam at his best for you!

I was star-struck at Goodison. I'd been watching the likes of Bob Latchford and Brian Kidd on the TV and was in awe of them.

But when I got over that I developed a bit of a chip on my shoulder. I had enjoyed a terrific rags to riches story and probably felt everything should happen quicker than it did at Everton.

I have to thank

# WITH A TOUCH OF MAGIC

Goodison coach Colin Harvey for knocking that out of me. I was taken under his wing and made to realise the value of patience. It paid off and I eventually made it into the first team.

The Everton boss, Gordon Lee, was a terrific manager and a great tactician. The trouble was understanding exactly who he was talking about. Gordon always got players' names mixed up. Team talks could be a laugh at times.

One memory of Gordon Lee always has me in stitches ... it had the boss in stitches, too! We were playing in Holland against Feyenoord in a UEFA Cup-tie.

I was on the substitutes bench. Just before kick-off we sat down but the boss was missing. Next minute he arrived with blood pouring from a head wound. Our physio had to go and patch him up.

The tunnel had a drawbridge-type door which closed when the teams were on the pitch. Apparently it had shut before Gordon could get out of the way!

My career at Everton might have been different if Gordon Lee had remained at Goodison. But I had just clocked up my best-ever consecutive run in any first team, when the boss was sacked and Howard Kendall took over.

He brought in seven new players straightaway and I couldn't see any future for myself from then on.

I then had the most exhilarating two years I have ever had in football! That was when I

signed for Newcastle United.

I had heard the stories about how the Geordie support loved a goal-scoring centre-forward. I had been warned, before I went to sign, about the pressure of wearing the black-and-white striped number nine jersey.

I've always worn the number nine shirt and I wasn't frightened to pull it on for Newcastle, but I had been made fully aware of the pressure on me.

Thankfully I scored goals — 20 in my first season — and didn't think things could get better. But then 'Keeganmania' hit Tyneside.

The signing of former England skipper Kevin Keegan was a real boost for the club. I've played in a few so-called hot-beds of soccer, Liverpool, Manchester and Sheffield. But nowhere buzzed like the city of Newcastle after Keegan's arrival.

I learnt a lot from playing alongside him. The main thing was enthusiasm for the game. Kevin was like a 16-year-old just starting out in football.

Between us we scored 43 goals in his debut season for Newcastle. I pipped him by a goal for the honour of top scorer. It had been a tremendous campaign and I was looking forward to the next one when it seemed as though we'd be certs for promotion to Division One.

The dream, however, collapsed around me in dramatic fashion. I was put up for sale that summer! I was absolutely shell-shocked.

I was saddened that such a brilliant two years had ended in such heartache. I have enjoyed keeping on the move in my career. I've always negotiated short contracts so that I was in control of my future.

Newcastle United was the one club where I would have liked to have stayed longer.

The Geordie fans, who had been so good to me in my two seasons up there, proved once more what a fanatical crowd they

are. After I left I received mountains of mail wishing me all the best and saying how shocked they had been that I was sold.

I'll never forget, either, the emotional reception they gave me when I faced them at Hillsborough for the first time after my transfer to Sheffield Wednesday.

Imprinted on my memory also are the thousands of stunned, silent faces which greeted me when I turned around after scoring at their end in that game! My Wednesday team-mates came up to me and kept telling me to celebrate, but I couldn't.

Sheffield Wednesday was a real experience. Howard Wilkinson was brilliant at man-management. His training methods are demanding. Many times we'd finish training sessions in the dark! And we've ploughed through deep snow in the Yorkshire hills on ten-mile runs.

I've known many varying training methods but Wednesday's were the most gruelling I've endured. However, it worked! We were happy to put the hours in because it suited the non-stop style favoured by Wednesday.

My feet began feeling itchy again after two seasons and I wound up at West Bromwich Albion. I signed for manager Johnny Giles and, although results weren't good, I was happy at the Hawthorns.

Giles resigned and myself and other senior players went to the chairman and requested that coach Nobby Stiles be installed as new boss. Nobby was reluctant but we got our wish and he took temporary charge.

Unfortunately the club later appointed Ron Saunders. I had a lot of disagreements with him so I was glad to get away and join Manchester City.

Maine Road is my sixth port of call — with my record it's doubtful if it will be my last!

51

**PAT NEVIN**
*Chelsea*

52

# SPURS' SECRET ARMY

## The behind-the-scene organisation of one of football's most famous clubs.

⚽ Once upon a time you could run a football club with a handful of helpers — a manager, coach, trainer, secretary and typist. Not any more. Not if Tottenham Hotspur Football Club is an example of a modern day outfit.

You see only eleven players at work on the pitch at White Hart Lane, but it takes a small army to get them out there fully fit, well coached and trained, well paid and well dressed. Nearly 100 people work at White Hart Lane every day — and none of them ever get to kick a ball!

Tottenham Hotspur is big business. The 51 players — 35 full-timers and 16 apprentices — account for only just over a third of the full-time employees. White Hart Lane is a business empire.

For instance, the name of Tottenham Hotspur is known around the world. There is a glamour about the club that is attractive to business men. The club recognised that fact when designing their new £5 million stand a few years ago.

Included in the new stand was a complex of suites that could be hired out to companies for meetings, presentations, lunches, Press conferences or dinner-dances. The Bill Nicholson Suite — named after the former manager — can seat up to 200 people.

A team of ten in the commercial office handle all the bookings and arrangements for the function rooms at White Hart Lane.

The commercial office also deals with ground advertising — up to £100,000 can be earned from a "live" television match — sponsorship deals (brewery giants Holsten are the overall club sponsors), and the letting of the 72 executive boxes.

Also handled by the commercial and marketing staff are sales of books — Spurs now publish their own titles under the Cockerel Books label — and

**MANAGER DAVID PLEAT — one of many important figures at White Hart Lane.**

home match video recordings.

Spurs are perhaps the only club in the league to run their own travel agency. At White Hart Lane you can book a day trip to Newcastle-upon-Tyne to watch a game or a 12,000 mile trip to Newcastle, New South Wales, for a holiday. A fully-trained and qualified staff of travel agents will arrange every detail of an overnight stop or the trip of a lifetime.

In the large Spurs shop you can buy almost anything in the famous dark blue and white colours, from pillow cases and pyjamas to posters and pens.

The Spurs shop also sells the "replica" kits as worn by the professionals. But at Tottenham there's a difference. The football club actually owns the UK division of the Danish firm Hummel which supplies the kit.

Tottenham became the national distributors of the brand last year, and now market a wide range of sportswear throughout the country.

Spurs also run their own restaurant, the Chanticleer, produce their own monthly newspaper called Spurs News, and run a number of special membership schemes.

At the top of the White Hart Lane pyramid is Chairman Irving Scholar. Under him, heading the different areas are Team Manager David Pleat, Secretary Peter Day, Financial Director Derek Peter, Commercial Manager Mike Rollo, Banqueting and Promotions Manager Denise Rowe, and Ticket Office Manager Chris Belt. Each one has their own team of assistants.

David Pleat has a coach, a reserve team manager, youth team manager, youth coach and two physiotherapists to help him. Plus a scouting staff of four, headed by former boss Bill Nicholson in a consultancy role, and two full-time kit men. In total, a staff of 13 on the football side.

Secretary Peter Day has an assistant, Peter Barnes, and nine administration staff backing him up. In the commercial department Mike Rollo and Denise Rowe have a staff of nine. Manager Harry Hughes heads a team of five in the Spurs Shop. In the ticket office, there are four helpers for manager Chris Belt.

There are three full-time security men, plus a special night staff, two full-time workers in the Travel Shop, four ground staff, plus casual workers, three laundry ladies, one tea lady, and one courier.

Programme Editor and PRO John Fennelly has an assistant to help him churn out articles for the match day magazines and the newspaper. The Hummel subsidiary employs around 20 workers marketing and despatching the clothing.

It all adds up to around 90 backroom staff at White Hart Lane — all playing a vital part in the running of a top football club.

# LIFE CAN BE TOUGH

## But it's worth it so

⚽ If there's one thing for sure about playing under manager Brian Clough at Nottingham Forest, it's that life is never predictable!

I've learned never to take anything for granted, because the moment I do that, the boss is liable to make a decision which will knock me sideways.

In just over two years at the City ground, those unexpected knock-backs have probably done me a world of good.

It's taught me not to start getting carried away, no matter how well things might be going on the field.

I'd only be setting myself up to be brought back down to earth with a bang, and Brian Clough is the right man to do just that. My earliest experience of this occurred two seasons ago, just after I began my run in the Forest first team.

We were playing a League match at West Ham United. Our goalkeeper, Hans Segers, was taken off injured after 20 minutes and I volunteered to take his place.

I conceded two goals in our 4-2 defeat, and you can imagine my dismay when I was dropped for our next fixture.

Mr Clough's public comment at the time was, 'He can't even play in midfield, let alone in goal.' Faced with that criticism, along with the embarrassment of being dropped, there were two paths open to me.

I could have given up hope and caved in altogether, or battled to show that I wasn't going to take things lying down.

I took the second of those routes, determinedly rolled up my sleeves for the fight, and won my place back within a week.

My second setback came at Easter in the same season. The boss told me that I hadn't been playing to my usual standard,

and dropped me for three matches. Again, I believe I earned a recall because I was so determined to prove him wrong.

Though it was no fun at the time, I look back now and realise that was probably Mr Clough's intention. He wanted to find out if I had the determination to fight back.

It's a technique which, I'm sure, must have aided the development of many a young player at Forest. Instead of too many allowances being made for youth, everybody is treated like an adult. After all, we're playing in a team, and each player has to pull his weight.

Mr Clough's approach encourages a mature attitude and builds character in his players. I certainly wouldn't have been shown up in a good light had I buckled when the pressure was on.

The current Forest team is made up predominantly of young players. I'm certain each of them can tell a similar story to my own, and all will have benefitted from Brian Clough's style of managership.

It can be a risky business relying heavily on youngsters. Over a season they can become tired or over-confident when they are doing well. But the boss has proved that he knows how to handle young players and keep getting the best out of them.

Of course, there are experienced players in the side, like Ian Bowyer and Garry Birtles, to help foster the right attitude.

Last season, for example, we had a tremendous start to the season, and forged to the top of the First Division. At one stage we were being hailed as the

Forest babes who were destined to win the title.

Some of us maybe started getting a little over confident, but Ian and Garry kept insisting that there was a long way to go and we shouldn't think too highly of ourselves.

They were proved correct, of course. Later in the season, we went through a sticky patch and dropped out of the race for the Championship. But we've learned from that experience and, hopefully, will become a better team in the future as a result.

As far as my own progress is concerned, I'm still learning. But in the last two years I've become a much better player, and made the full England squad for several international fixtures. I'm the first to acknowledge that the guidance I've received from Brian Clough has been a major influence.

Having been moved around in four different positions with my previous club, Portsmouth, I was given a chance at Forest to settle down in my best role — the centre of midfield.

Brian Clough didn't put any restrictions on me. I was left to get up and down the field doing my share of attacking and defending.

In the process, I've achieved a high level of consistency. Previously that had always been my main failing. Until signing for Forest, I'd turn in a good performance one week and a mediocre one the next.

Having said that, I still believe

that I chose the correct route into top-class football when I signed as a 16-year-old apprentice for my local club, Reading.

A lot of my mates had been signing for top First Division outfits on schoolboy forms. At that time, Reading were playing in the Third Division.

However, I made the first team when I was still 16, and by the time I moved to Portsmouth I had more than 80 senior matches under my belt.

That gave me much more experience than all those lads who were still plugging away in the youth teams of bigger clubs.

Playing against seasoned professionals week after week, I grew up the hard way, but definitely the best way. If I had my time over again, I'd do exactly the same.

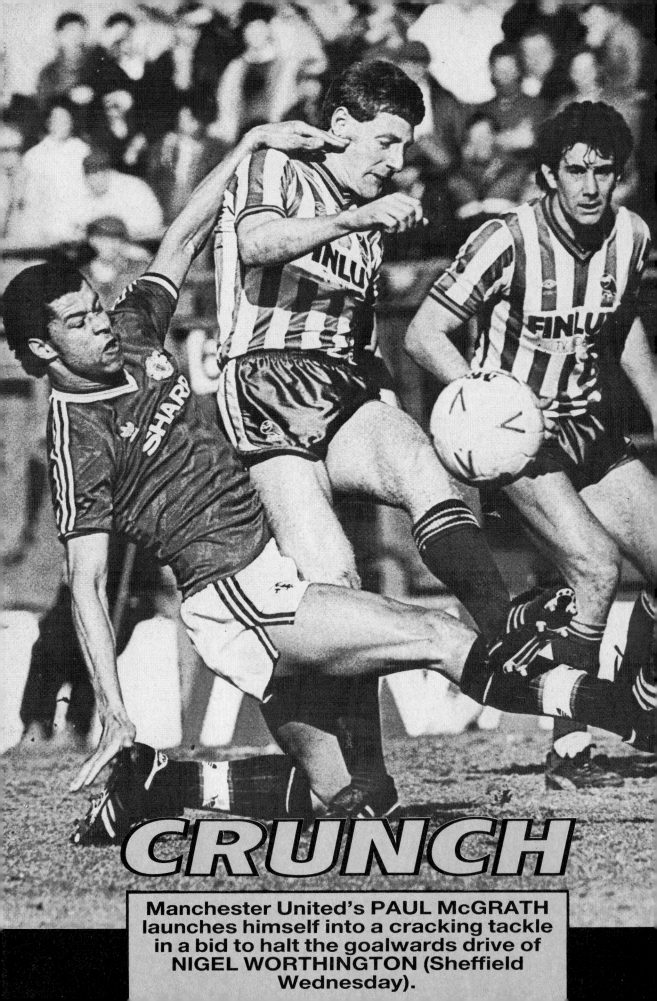

# CRUNCH

**Manchester United's PAUL McGRATH launches himself into a cracking tackle in a bid to halt the goalwards drive of NIGEL WORTHINGTON (Sheffield Wednesday).**

JIM BETT
*Aberdeen*

59

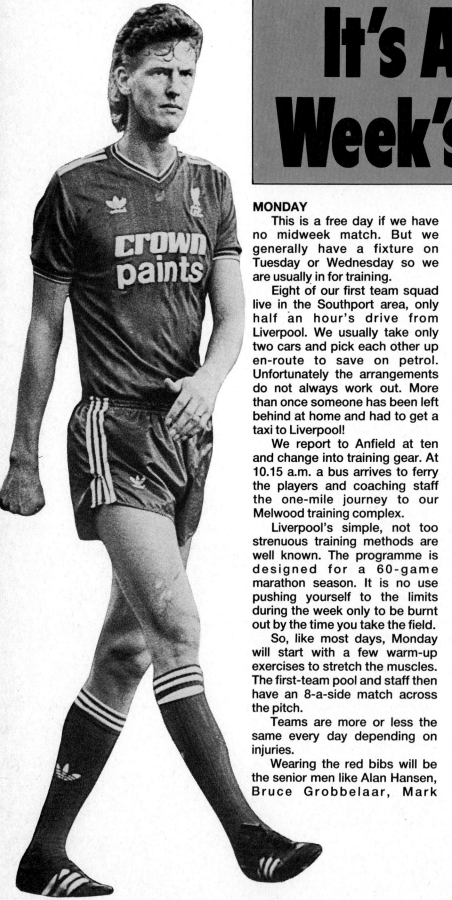

# It's All In A Week's Work

## MONDAY

This is a free day if we have no midweek match. But we generally have a fixture on Tuesday or Wednesday so we are usually in for training.

Eight of our first team squad live in the Southport area, only half an hour's drive from Liverpool. We usually take only two cars and pick each other up en-route to save on petrol. Unfortunately the arrangements do not always work out. More than once someone has been left behind at home and had to get a taxi to Liverpool!

We report to Anfield at ten and change into training gear. At 10.15 a.m. a bus arrives to ferry the players and coaching staff the one-mile journey to our Melwood training complex.

Liverpool's simple, not too strenuous training methods are well known. The programme is designed for a 60-game marathon season. It is no use pushing yourself to the limits during the week only to be burnt out by the time you take the field.

So, like most days, Monday will start with a few warm-up exercises to stretch the muscles. The first-team pool and staff then have an 8-a-side match across the pitch.

Teams are more or less the same every day depending on injuries.

Wearing the red bibs will be the senior men like Alan Hansen, Bruce Grobbelaar, Mark Lawrenson and, of course player-manager Kenny Dalglish. Trainers Ronnie Moran and Roy Evans make up the numbers.

The yellow side is made up of the younger lads such as Barry Venison, Ronnie Whelan, Paul Walsh, Nigel Spackman and myself.

Honours generally work out fairly even over a week. Nobody goes in hard. Challenges are made cautiously to avoid injuring anyone.

After about half an hour, the boss will break up the game and we'll have a spell of sprints. To finish the morning off there will be another short practice match. The session ends around noon.

The coach then takes us back to Anfield where we bath and get changed. The lads then drift into the club canteen for a light lunch. Bacon and eggs and beans on toast are the favourites on the menu.

After lunch, the afternoon and evening are free. If we have a mid-week fixture, the advice is normally to put your feet up and save as much energy as possible. Snooker and golf are the most popular spare-time activities.

Some afternoons and evenings are taken up visiting hospitals to boost morale of patients or going to schools to present prizes at functions.

Those players with sponsored cars often make personal appearances at the dealer's garage to sign autographs.

## TUESDAY

Pattern very similar to Monday except the training session is stepped up a bit.

Lunch at Anfield at 1.00 p.m., before leaving for away destination some time during the afternoon.

After travelling by coach to the hotel the evening meal is taken at 6.00 p.m. Chicken, fish or steak is normally the choice. Only midfielder Craig Johnston has any special requirements.

In recent years Craig has become hooked on the high fibre diet favoured by successful tennis stars Ivan Lendl and Martina Navratilova. Not that Craig is attempting to lose weight, but the rice and pasta based dishes he now prefers are designed to give you instant energy.

Evenings are free — the hotel pool table or TV lounge are in demand. By 9.30 p.m. we are in bed.

## WEDNESDAY

Match day. We have a light breakfast around 8.30 a.m., then at ten o'clock travel by coach to a pre-arranged local training ground. Just a very easy loosener as the game is now only hours away.

Return to hotel at noon and have lunch. We retire to our beds in the afternoon. Most of us try to get in a few hours' sleep.

5.00 p.m. Alarm call and into hotel restaurant for a light evening meal. Tea, toast, scrambled egg and jam are allowed. Nothing too substantial at this stage of the day.

6.00 p.m. Coach ride to stadium. After arranging complimentary tickets for family and friends, the squad shut themselves in the dressing-room and go through individual pre-match routines.

When the room is plunged into darkness we know that goalkeeper Bruce Grobbelaar has finished his ritual. Bruce will kick a football against a light switch until he turns the lights off.

Thankfully he's pretty good at it these days so we don't have to wait too long until he's finished!

An hour to kick-off and manager Kenny Dalglish will announce his line-up. It is only then that we'll have a discussion about the game and the opposition.

7.30-9.10 p.m. The match. After the game there are usually Press and radio interviews to be done.

Around 10.00 p.m. we're back on the road again and heading for Liverpool. Prior arrangements are always made for us to stop en-route at a chip shop. The driver will collect the 16 or so fish and chip suppers which will be consumed on the coach. Yes, it's true, Liverpool eating out of newspaper!

We return to Anfield, collect our cars and then drive home.

## THURSDAY

Having had a match the night previous we do not go into Anfield until midday. There we all have a hot bath and a long soak for half an hour or more. After that we have lunch at the ground and then the afternoon is our own.

## FRIDAY

Normal routine. Training is stepped up considerably after doing nothing the day before. It's a question of getting the legs going again.

Even if you are injured, if you are capable of doing something, then you have to attend training sessions. Those with injuries may just walk or jog around the track, but the club likes us to be together whenever possible.

Treatment on injuries starts after lunch.

## SATURDAY

Arrive at Anfield at 11.30 a.m. for Saturday home match. Then bus takes us to a Liverpool city centre hotel. Menu for the pre-match meal is similar to the lunchtime prior to an evening game. However, as the match is that few hours closer, there is a ban on potatoes and chips.

The hotel TV lounge will then be packed and often resounding with derisive laughter as we watch the football programmes! We'll stick around for a couple of televised horse-races before leaving for the ground at 1.30 p.m.

After a Saturday game we let our hair down in the evening. Generally it's a drink and a meal with wives and girlfriends.

## SUNDAY

The only real fry-up breakfast of the week!

It's also often our only full day at home. So, apart from a game of golf some weekends, I tend to spend as much of it as I can with the family.

And that rounds off one more week — Liverpool style!

**ENERGY SEEKER — diet - conscious Craig Johnston.**

**STEVE GRITT**
*Charlton*

62

**GARY MEGSON**
*Sheffield Wednesday*

65

# It's Been Wonderfu

⚽ I've had some great years with Wimbledon since I joined them from Edgware Town but none could top last season — our first in Division One. I'd always hoped to play in the top flight and last year my dream came true after coming all the way up through the league with Wimbledon.

It was a very special day for the club when we travelled up to Maine Road to play our first-ever Division One match against Manchester City. We'd played there before while in the Second Division but this game was a great day for Wimbledon and all the players.

Unfortunately we lost that day but nothing could spoil the occasion. Our former manager, Dave Bassett, had always told me I was capable of playing in Division One — and there I was!

It was all very different from the days when I played non-League with Edgware Town in North London. That was where Wimbledon found me. Dave Bassett was assistant to manager Dario Gradi then and he was the one who came to see me play.

When I heard that he was there, I rushed out of the dressing-room still in my playing-kit to see him. I was so keen to talk to somebody from a league club, even if Wimbledon were only in the Fourth Division at the time. But Dave told me to go back and wait until he had permission from my club to talk to me.

Thankfully nobody stood in my way, so I was soon heading for Plough Lane. It was only a year or so later Dave Bassett became manager and we haven't really looked back since. Even though we're now in the First Division, a lot of things are just the same at the club. Dave laid down a routine when he took over and it didn't change much while he was in charge. Pre-season training is definitely just as hard, if not harder, than it ever was. But even if it is hard work, I

## That's the view of long-serving goalkeeper DAVE BEASANT

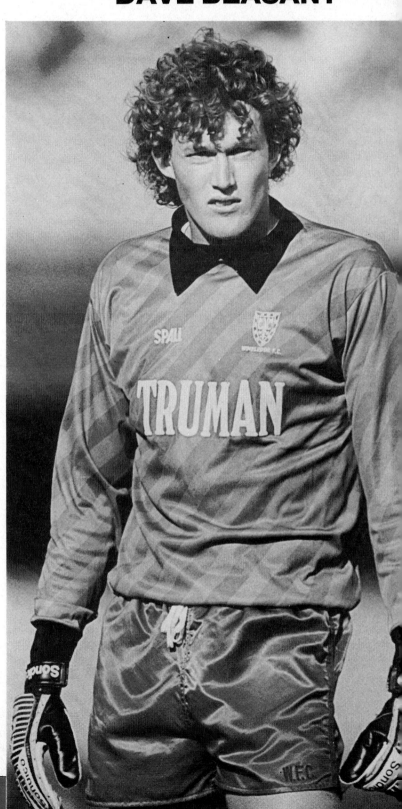

# t Wimbledon!

still enjoy the way we prepare for each new campaign.

A feature of pre-season training in recent times has been our work with the army. In the last few years we've joined up for a week of intensive training in camps both in this country and in Germany.

By the end of a week with the army we're all very fit and raring to go for the season. And by the end of the year all that extra training really shows its worth because we're much fitter than most sides.

When we've finished at the army camp we get on with some ballwork. For a goalkeeper such as myself that often means a trip up to Lilleshall to train with goalkeeping coach Mike Kelly. He's in charge of the England keepers for international games and I find it very useful to work with him three or four times a season. The coaching staff at Wimbledon are excellent but here is no specialist goalkeeping coach.

It's very good for me to go up and see Mike and he has encouraged me to take coaching badges myself, so that when I hang up my gloves I'll be able to do some coaching work.

Although I've learnt a lot from Mike Kelly, it was the physio at Wimbledon, Derek French, who proved to be a big help in one important area of my game — goal-kicking. Derek noticed that I had been slicing my drop-kicks to the right and losing distance as a result. He said that I was lifting my head when I kicked and it had the same effect as slicing a golf shot. After straightening out that problem my goal-kicks became an important part of our game — and my golf improved as well!

As my goal-kicks got better and better, I started to claim regular "assists" in a lot of our goals by placing the ball on the head of one of our tall strikers. But that's far from being my only involvement with the outfield play. I've always been quite

**HE SET WIMBLEDON ON THE WINNING WAY —**
**ex-manager Dave Bassett.**

confident with the ball at my feet because I used to be a striker, and I quite often come out of my area to play like a sweeper.

I'm also in charge of taking nearly all the free-kicks in our half. Some people think I'm a bit eccentric but I just like to be involved in the game, which is very important as captain.

It was playing our own way that helped us to achieve so much last season, the highlights of which were to become the subject of a B.B.C. documentary. The cameras had followed us to Maine Road for that first game of the season just to do a short piece for Football Focus, but they were so impressed with what they saw that they decided to make a full programme. There would certainly be some great moments for them to capture throughout the season.

The best of all came against two of the top teams — Everton and Liverpool. In the early part of the season both the Merseyside teams came to Plough Lane and beat us and just before Christmas we suffered a 3-0 defeat at Goodison Park. But we were to get our revenge!

We met Everton in the fifth round of the F.A. Cup. Although

we were at home, nobody fancied our chances much. We soon went behind but then we fought back to score a famous 3-1 win. It was a great day for everybody at Wimbledon and it was all captured on TV.

Unfortunately, there weren't any cameras around to film the best moment of all in our first season in the top flight. That was the day we went to Anfield and beat the reigning champions on their home ground. It was a victory we fully deserved. I've had some great times with Wimbledon, but it would be hard to match that one.

When we topped the table for ten days in the first part of the season, nobody took us seriously. However, by the time we'd beaten Liverpool at Anfield, I think everybody realised we could play football.

For me that win at Liverpool was a fantastic climax to six seasons in which I hadn't missed a single game. By avoiding injury and suspension I'd managed to play in every game on our incredible journey from the Fourth to the First Division., It took me nearly 300 League games to get to Anfield — but it was certainly well worth the wait.

67

**BRIAN KILCLINE**
*Coventry City*

68

ALAN McDONALD
Queens Park Rangers

# NIGHTMARE

Southampton's GLENN COCKERI
remembers the 7-0 thrashing tha
was his First Division baptism.

⚽ I can remember very clearly the night that changed my career. But I wasn't playing in or even watching the match concerned. The occasion was the last game of the 1983-84 season. Hull City were playing away at Burnley in a Third Division game.

If Hull managed to win 3-0 they would be promoted instead of my new club, Sheffield United. I'd joined United from Lincoln in the March of 1984 and played the last ten games of the season.

On the last Saturday of the season we'd beaten Newport, but Hull could only draw with Bristol Rovers. That put us three points clear but Hull could still beat us on goal difference.

It was one of the most nerve-racking experiences of my life waiting for that result to come in from Burnley. I switched on the teletext on my television and it flashed up the news that Brian Marwood had put Hull 1-0 up. And when Marwood scored again just after half-time I thought our hopes of promotion had gone. I couldn't watch any more, so I went for a walk.

When I came back I turned on the teletext. I couldn't believe my eyes when I saw that the score had remained at 2-0, which meant we were promoted.

That night really did have a big influence on my career. If Hull had scored more goals I would have stayed in Division Three, where I'd played most of my football. But the step-up to the Second Division was ultimately to give me the chance to play in Division One.

My football career had, in fact, started off at a much lower level than Division Three. When I was just fifteen I played my first senior football for Midland League Louth United. During the day I had jobs such as heating engineer and factory dustman but in the evenings and on Saturday afternoons I could do what I really wanted to do — play football. Although I played for Louth's first team, I was still

70

young enough to play for the junior side as well and it was in one such game that I came up against Lincoln City juniors.

Graham Taylor was manager of Lincoln at the time, just before he moved on to Watford, and after seeing me in that junior game he invited me for a trial spell at Lincoln. I was initially taken on for six weeks, and then for the rest of the season. And while Graham was still there he taught me all the right things about the game.

Lincoln was a very good nursery for young players. You could probably make up a full team from those who have graduated from Sincil Bank to the First Division. John Fashanu has made a name for himself with Wimbledon, Trevor Peake played in the Cup Final for Coventry, Gordon Hobson is now a team-mate of mine at Southampton and Mick Harford is a top class centre-forward with Luton.

Mick Harford actually started his career as a midfielder and I played up front. It was only after we swapped positions that we both started to make real progress. But, like me, Mick had to make a few moves until he found his way into the top flight.

My first transfer from Lincoln took me to Swindon where the manager was Bobby Smith, who unfortunately didn't stay in the job long after I arrived. And the bad news for me was that his successor, John Trollope, didn't want me in the team.

It didn't seem like it at the time, but that spell at Swindon, some of which was spent in the reserves, did me a lot of good. I was soon bought back by Lincoln and I felt that I was returning as a better player. It might have seemed a strange move to go back to my old club but I still saw it as a step-up at that stage of my career. And it was certainly my form in that second spell at Lincoln which made Sheffield United interested in me.

When I finally stepped up to the Second Division, I had high hopes that United might go straight through to win promotion to the First. There were players in the team with a lot of top flight experience, such as Peter Withe, Phil Thompson and Ken McNaught. But although we began quite well, things started going wrong and we finished the season in 18th place — much closer to relegation than to promotion.

There was tremendous support at Bramall Lane and the fans were desperate to get back into the First Division alongside their neighbours Sheffield Wednesday. But unfortunately we didn't quite live up to their expectations. It all looked good on paper but we rarely had a settled side and you can't hope to do well without that.

Thankfully I'd managed to play more games than anyone else that season which gave me plenty of opportunities to be seen by First Division clubs. During the next summer it looked as if I was all set to join Luton Town, but for some reason that move fell through and I found myself starting another season with United in the Second Division.

I played the first dozen games and things went much better than before. But then the moment I'd been waiting for finally arrived when I signed for Southampton. I'd probably played the best football of my career at Sheffield United but now I knew I was set for the real test in Division One.

I couldn't have made a worse start at Southampton, however. My first game for the Saints was away from home at Luton. Manager Chris Nicholl played me up front in that game so that I could ease my way into the side, but I hardly saw anything of the ball.

The man who did see plenty of the action was Peter Shilton. We were thrashed 7-0 that day by a rampant Luton side that included my old Lincoln team-mate, Mick Harford. It really was a nightmare start but I didn't let it worry me for long, especially as we started on a very good run of results after that awful defeat.

Southampton haven't exactly had a lot of success over the last two years but I've personally enjoyed every minute of my period in the First Division. I waited a long time to play at the top level and I was determined to make the most of my chance when it finally came. And there have been a few highlights along the way.

In my first season with the club we got to the semi-final of the F.A. Cup against Liverpool at White Hart Lane. We played very well that day but in the end we were beaten in extra-time by two Ian Rush goals after our central defender Mark Wright had broken his leg.

Then last season we again lost to Liverpool when just one step away from Wembley — in the Littlewoods Cup. So this season I'll be hoping that it's a case of third time lucky for me.

**MICK HARFORD — striking top form for Luton Town.**

**DAVE WATSON**
*Everton*

72

**BILLY GILBERT**
*Portsmouth*

73

# SOMETHING TO CELEBRATE!

## The Football League is 100 years old — and still going strong!

The Football League was founded on April 17th, 1888. Then there were 12 clubs. Now there are 92 making it the largest professional league in world football.

The League grew to 14 clubs within three years and inside another year it had 28 clubs in two divisions; at the same time promotion and relegation were introduced.

Things progressed at such a pace that, by the turn of the century, League football had grown into the biggest spectator sport in the country. It still is — despite all the counter attractions.

After the First World War, the Football League more than doubled its membership to four divisions of 22 clubs each. Four more clubs were added in 1950-51 increasing the lower two divisions, the League's associate members, to 24 clubs each.

The League will go into its Centenary season with the First Division decreased to 21 clubs. By the start of the 1988-89 season the League's planned new format of 20 clubs in the First Division and 24 in each of the Second, Third and Fourth Divisions will be complete.

In 1960-61 the League launched its own knock-out cup competition. Three seasons ago, the associate members of the League introduced their own knock-out cup (the Freight Rover Trophy). A year later the First and Second Division clubs followed suit, with the introduction of the Full Members' Cup. So now the Football League is responsible for more than 2,500 matches a season.

The League inspired a multi-million pound industry when the football pools began in the mid-twenties. Now football is in the forefront of the sponsorship explosion. Football's partnership with industry in the eighties ranges from multi-million pound sponsorships such as the Today League and the Littlewoods Challenge Cup to substantial club sponsorships and even to individual match sponsorships.

In the beginning, matches were played on small grounds, and with limited seating. Now we are in the era of sophisticated stadia — though the League's record attendance figure of 82,950 for the Manchester United v. Arsenal match in 1947-48 is hardly likely to be surpassed.

Full-backs, half-backs and forwards have become defenders, midfield men and strikers. Substitutes, introduced in 1965, are now part and parcel of a manager's playing strategy.

The changing of the offside law in 1925 brought a new dimension to League football. The goals flooded in. At least they did until the late Herbert Chapman, the manager who guided Huddersfield to three successive League titles in the twenties, gave the matter some thought.

By then, Chapman was manager of Arsenal. He "created" the stopper centre-half playing between the two full backs. Arsenal's defence seemed impregnable and the club equalled Huddersfield's feat of a hat-trick of Championships.

Without doubt, Chapman was then the most successful manager in the history of the League. He was to be challenged in the immediate post-war years by Matt Busby, who inherited a Manchester United club without

## SPECIAL OCCASIONS THAT MARK A FAMOUS MILESTONE

This is the glittering array of events, sponsored by Mercantile Credit, which the Football League has had arranged to make sure everyone can share in the celebrations.

### August 7th, 1987
### CENTENARY DINNER

An international occasion with a star-studded guest list of more than 1,000 people — representatives of international football authorities, overseas football leagues and associations, the 92 League clubs and many world-famous football personalities, both past and present.

### August 8th, 1987
### CENTENARY CLASSIC
### (Wembley Stadium)

Bobby Robson, the England manager, and Terry Venables, the Barcelona manager, select teams representing the Football League and the Rest of the World.

### September 20th, 1987
### CENTENARY FUN RUN

League football's own campaign in aid of local charities. On that day, each League club stages a two-and-a-half mile sponsored Centenary Fun Run in conjunction with local authorities.

Players and supporters alike of every League club set out in their tens of thousands from 92 venues throughout England and Wales.

### October 1st, 1987
### CENTENARY GALA CONCERT
### (Royal Albert Hall, London)

A show business tribute to football. A glittering occasion with a "surprise" international star.

### November 25th, 1987
### CENTENARY CHALLENGE

Scottish players have made a special contribution to English club football over the past 100 years. The Centenary Challenge match will bring together the respective champions of the English and Scottish Leagues.

### April 13th to 16th, 1988
### CENTENARY FESTIVAL CONCERTS
### (Wembley Arena)

Forty thousand pop fans join the League's birthday celebrations during a four-night festival of pop music. The Festival Concerts will see top rock groups giving their own salute to football.

### April 16th, 17th, 1988
### CENTENARY FESTIVAL
### (Wembley Stadium)

The birth-date of League football was April 17th, 1888. Precisely 100 years later, The Football League will stage a full weekend festival of football with all 92 League clubs competing in a six-a-side tournament.

### August 6th, 10th and 13th, 1988
### CENTENARY TROPHY

A knockout competition featuring the clubs who finish in the top eight places in the First Division of the Today League in season 1987-88.

Each round will be on a single leg basis with clubs seeded according to their previous season's League position.

All matches will be played at League grounds, with the Final being staged at a neutral venue.

---

a grandstand or a playable pitch.

Busby created the "Busby Babes", legends in their tragically short lifetimes. Manchester United, under Busby's guidance, became the team everybody wanted to see.

Busby and United reigned during the late forties and fifties. With Busby in charge, United became the first club from the Football League to win the European Cup. Liverpool subsequently won that trophy four times.

The Anfield club have also won the League Championship 16 times, twice as many as their nearest rivals, Everton and Arsenal. Eleven of those title successes have come since 1964, no fewer than eight of them in the last 11 seasons.

Football League clubs have a remarkable success story in European competitions. Nottingham Forest won the European Cup twice, Aston Villa

won it once. And the U.E.F.A. and Cup Winners' Cups were brought home regularly from Europe by other League clubs, such as Liverpool, Leeds, Chelsea, Spurs, Ipswich, Newcastle and Manchester City.

Football remains the nation's number one sporting interest and the Football League remains the strongest and broadest-based professional league in the world. The first hundred years are a history to be proud of.

**BRYAN GUNN**
*Norwich City*

# HOW THE MONEY ROLLS IN....

**For most clubs, the money generated at the turnstiles is not enough to make ends meet. Other sources of revenue are a must — and that's where commercial managers have their part to play. It's up to them to come up with ideas on how to raise money. Here are just some of the ways that different commercial managers face up to the challenge.**

## PHIL CRITCHLEY (Manchester City)

In the same way as shops run Christmas clubs so do some football clubs. We have such a venture going.

Fans can save up each week for their Christmas hamper. At Maine Road we sold £100,000 worth of hampers last festive season. We also added to the range by introducing jewellery.

Young couples can save with us for their engagement and wedding rings, for instance. It isn't an enormous money-maker for us but it does serve the purpose of getting people involved with City.

Like many other clubs we are also involved in the British Telecom Clubcall. Fans phone the special line for information and gossip items on City. We receive a small percentage on the volume of calls.

We have a Luncheon Club at Maine Road, with one hundred members paying a certain amount per year. For that they are given a lunch every month when they can each invite a guest. We provide a guest speaker. In the past we've had top names from sport, politics and showbusiness.

The funds from the latter venture are specifically set aside for the development of young players.

## KEITH HANVEY (Huddersfield Town)

Three years ago the club organised a "Walking for Town" event. We were playing at Blackburn, a distance of around 30 miles away. Fans were sponsored to walk from our ground at Leeds Road to Ewood Park.

Two hundred supporters made the trip on foot, timing it so they arrived for the Saturday afternoon kick-off. It was an incredible event and certainly a good money spinner. We've not asked the fans to undertake such a foot-slogging trek since, but their training shoes get a regular hammering on our fun runs.

Our golf classics have been another popular event. Teams are entered by pubs, clubs, companies, etc. who have to pay a fee to enter. Proceeds — after prize money — go to Huddersfield.

Similarly with the race nights. Video films of horseraces from America are shown and bets are laid on the outcome. We've also had a few sponsored darts nights.

## DAVID PULLAN (Nottingham Forest)

At Forest we run an Executive Club with 250 members. For an annual fee they are invited to regular, prize draw cabaret evenings at a top hotel in Nottingham.

Each member and his guest are dined free of charge and have the chance to win such items as gold watches, drinks cabinets and Forest season tickets.

For the big evening of the year the top prize was a cruise! The club has generated great interest and revenue.

As we are just a minute's walk from the Trent Bridge cricket ground we also utilise our 36 executive boxes at the City Ground when there is a Test match on.

A box is rented out for the duration of the Test. The eight people in each box are given morning coffee and biscuits on arrival at Forest and are then escorted across to watch the cricket. They return to the football ground for lunch and we supply an entertainer. It brings in revenue during the summer when the boxes would otherwise be unused.

We try to use the ground as much as we can. We had 12,000 attend a Jehovah's Witness convention and due soon are an American grid-iron football team from Hawaii. They've issued a challenge to local American football side Mansfield Express. It's a good family day out and we are expecting 25,000 at the ground.

## ALAN HARDY (Oldham Athletic)

In 1986 we launched the Blue Bond club at Boundary Park. It has been an enormous success. We doubled our break even figure in the first few weeks. Fans pay a weekly subscription of 50p. For that they have a chance of winning £100 in each daily prize draw.

On top of that we have arranged for discounts with local and national companies on certain products on production of a club membership card.

Supporters can get money off a wide range of goods ranging from double-glazing, fitted kitchens and bathrooms to clothes, gardening equipment and car servicing.

There are chances, too, to win holidays. In the first month after the scheme was announced, 6,000 people applied to join.

It was a fantastic response, but it's not easy coming up with new ideas for fund raising. Grabbing the public's imagination is becoming more difficult.

But these are not the only examples of commercial managers coming up with bright ideas. Here are a few of the ways other clubs have found to boost their finances.

## QUEEN'S PARK RANGERS

*Queen's Park Rangers boosted lottery ticket sales at Loftus Road with a unique offer. They guaranteed the use of their artificial pitch to any local club or junior team who could sell 1500 lottery tickets.*

*Any side reaching that target could book the Rangers pitch and other facilities for private matches free of charge. Rangers were inundated with requests to sell tickets — and many clubs reached their target.*

## SOUTHAMPTON

The medal winning team in Southampton these days doesn't play at the Dell — but sometimes they run round it.

The nucleus of Britain's medal-winning 400 metres men's athletics squad is based in Southampton. And the football club's astute commercial manager Bob Britten has made use of that fact.

As an attraction at the Dell he invited the relay squad to stage some pre-match races involving European 400 metre champion Roger Black and his colleagues Todd Bennett and Kris Akabusi.

The athletics stars ran some exhibition races and also invited fans to run against them. All aimed at adding to the attendance at the Dell and keeping fans entertained.

*ROGER BLACK*

## LUTON TOWN

Luton Town used to have the biggest electronic scoreboard in the country, before replacing it with two smaller screens, one at each end of the ground.

The big screen was perfect for selling advertising space before games, or at half-time. But the most memorable message was no advert — it was a marriage proposal! A Luton fan approached the club and asked if he could propose to his girlfriend at a first team match via the electronic scoreboard.

Television's "That's Life" programme got to hear of the plan and sent a camera team to Kenilworth Road to record the event. The astonished girl friend could hardly believe it when she read the "Will you marry me?" message before the kick-off.

She recovered her composure to send the answer at half-time. And her "yes" message got the biggest cheer of the day.

## WEST HAM UNITED

West Ham United, the team from London's East End, were not slow to spot the opportunity when the BBC's soap EastEnders was a nationwide hit. The football club linked up with stars from the show on a number of occasions both for charity and for club fund raising efforts.

Leslie Grantham — "Dirty Den" — has become a familiar face at Upton Park presenting lottery winners with cheques. In addition, most of the Albert Square cast have become West Ham fans.

## WATFORD

*Watford have a lively and inventive commercial department at Vicarage Road. One of their money-spinners is to sell advertising space on the electronic score-board during matches. Even fans can buy space. For £10, supporters can wish "Mum" a Happy Birthday.*

*But for £350 Watford supporters could give Mum — or themselves — a special treat. A flight on Concorde! Members of Watford's "Top Draw" promotional scheme have a variety of special offers to take advantage of — a trip to the Grand National, a champagne journey on the famous Orient Express train, or the Supersonic flight on Concorde.*

79

JOHN LUKIC
Arsenal

 **JOHN GREGORY**
*Derby County*

# MY PASSPORT

⚽ Most people in this country probably take their British passports for granted. I'm sure that, for the greater part of the year, they are left lying in a drawer, taken out for foreign holidays, then forgotten again.

Not mine. When the envelope containing my own passport dropped though my letter-box last year, it was the most welcome delivery the postman could possibly have made.

Receiving that document was one of the most important things to have happened to me since I came to England to play football six years ago.

It arrived at a time when I was

beginning to achieve some of my international football ambitions, but had been frustrated on occasions because I didn't have British citizenship.

After five years of waiting, it meant that finally, when England Under-21 team manager Dave Sexton asked me if I was available for European Championship duty, I was able to say, 'Yes.'

Previously, I'd been allowed to appear only in friendly matches. But whenever a competitive fixture came along, I was automatically ruled out.

The reason for those problems was that I was born in Australia. Yet, having lived in

England since 1981, I now think of it as my own country.

Though I had the chance to play for Australia in the World Cup even before being considered for the England Under-21 side, I turned it down. My international ambitions are solely restricted to pulling on an England shirt.

In fact, ever since I was 12 years old, I've wanted to play top-class football in this country.

I was already playing senior football in Australia. Having achieved first team status with Adelaide City at 15, I'd become the youngest player ever to turn out for the club. I was also told I may even have been the youngest to play for a senior club in Australia.

At that stage I reckoned it was time to discover just how much further I could progress in my football career.

So I wrote to 12 English First Division clubs, asking for a trial. Only two replied. Manchester United wrote to say sorry, but they were unable to take me at that time. Aston Villa, however, invited me to join them for a four-day trial.

Of course, I was taking a gamble. So my father decided to travel over here with me — especially as I'd never been out of Australia before.

I must have done well during that initial four-day trial, because Villa kept extending my trying-out period. Finally, after four weeks, they agreed to sign me on schoolboy forms.

However, there were several drawbacks I had to face before I could come to terms with my new life, and I almost gave up my quest for big-time football.

For one thing, Villa had to send me back to school for six months. I thought I'd left that behind when I finished my schooling in Australia.

There, the leaving age is 15. However, kids in Britain must

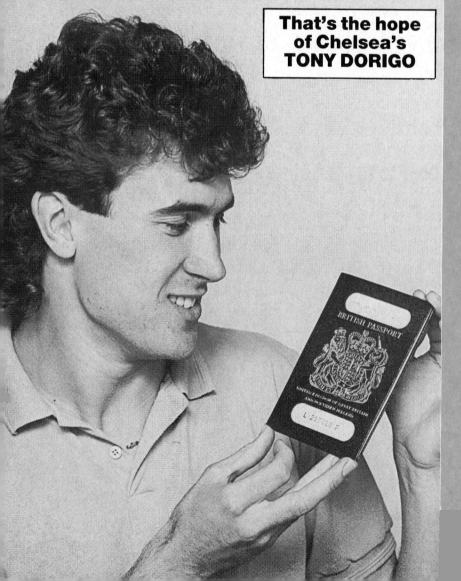

That's the hope of Chelsea's TONY DORIGO

remain at school until they are 16, so I had to conform to that ruling.

It was frustrating to spend those six months wrapped up in schoolbooks again, when all I wanted to do was work at improving my football.

Additionally, I was staying at a Villa hostel with other boys of a similar age. But they were able to go home at the weekends to be with their families. I had to stay behind on my own. Those months were very lonely ones.

At the end of my first six months, the football season ended, and so did the school year, so I packed my bags and went home for seven weeks. I almost didn't come back!

That first spell in England had been so hard for me, I seriously considered giving it all up and settling back into a normal family life. I spent the whole seven weeks trying to make a decision.

My family were wonderful. They constantly offered advice that finally convinced me I should persevere at Villa.

They all said that if I gave up at that point, I would never forgive myself. That settled the issue — and of course, they have since been proved right.

Life became a lot easier on my return to Britain. Villa signed me as an apprentice and, with no school to worry about, I was able to concentrate totally on training and playing football.

Though I was still living in the hostel, my family had already started making plans to emigrate from Australia and set up home in England just to be with me.

I made good progress. At 17½, I became a full professional and was turning out regularly for the reserve side.

In mid-1983 my family — mum, dad and younger sister Lisa — arrived, so I moved in with them. Being together again seemed to have a beneficial effect on my football.

Very soon the England Youth team manager phoned Villa to ask if I was available for international duty. It was that enquiry which first sparked off my quest for a British passport.

My application was turned down, and we were informed that I'd have to be resident in this country for five years before I could be granted a passport.

In the meantime, I would be allowed to play in friendly matches for the international side. But, as the youth side were involved in the European Championship tournament at that time, I was ruled out of these games.

However, Aston Villa chairman Doug Ellis then stepped in. Despite the five-year regulation, he ensured an application was sent into the passport office every six months, so that the authorities were constantly aware of my position.

Meanwhile, my career at club level was going from strength to strength. I made my first team debut, aged 18, coming on as a substitute against Ipswich Town on the final day of the 1983-84 season.

In the following campaign, I became a regular first-teamer and have missed only a handful of matches in the last couple of years.

Just as I was establishing myself in the senior team, the Australian FA contacted me to ask if I'd be interested in playing for their national side. At that time, they were involved in the qualifying stages of the 1986 World Cup.

However, I felt it wasn't really practical for me to accept their offer. It would have meant taking a three-month break from English football, which I couldn't afford because I was still trying to make a name for myself at Villa Park.

Besides, having spent a few

years in England, I'd come to regard this as my new country, and I felt I might have an international future with England.

This was confirmed when Dave Sexton, the Under-21 manager, contacted me at the start of last season to ask if I was available for his side.

Again, I had to explain the problem about my passport qualifications. Fortunately, the match he was preparing for was a friendly in Sweden, so I was able to join the squad, and ended up in the match line-up.

The next few weeks were full of disappointments and thrills.

Mr Sexton rang again, saying that he was working out his squad for the next match, a European Championship fixture against Yugoslavia. He wanted to know if my passport had arrived. My five-year wait was almost up.

Unfortunately, I'd still heard nothing. I felt dejected when Mr Sexton was forced to tell me, 'I'm sorry, but I won't be able to pick you.'

Two days later, my despair turned to joy when that official envelope dropped through my letter box. My passport was in it.

It came just in time for the Yugoslavia game and I was invited to join the squad after all. But, as Nottingham Forest's Stuart Pearce had already been drafted in as an over-age player, he was handed the number three jersey. At least I managed to get a seat on the substitutes' bench.

After that, however, I became a regular in the Under-21 side. It was marvellous to be able to declare myself available whenever a squad was being announced.

Now I'm looking to earning promotion to Bobby Robson's full England team.

After all that I've been through during the last six years, there's no way I'll settle for anything less than the top.

high flyer!

Norwich City's WAYNE
BIGGINS takes to the air
— helped in take-off by
the sliding tackle of West
Ham's TONY GALE

# RESTORED TO GLORY!

## The story behind one of football's most sought-after trophies — the Littlewoods Cup.

When Arsenal beat Liverpool at Wembley in the Littlewoods Cup Final last season, they became the first winners under the new sponsor's name. But when Gunners' captain Kenny Sansom led his team up to the Royal Box, he received what is believed to be the oldest existing football trophy in the world.

The impressive solid silver trophy, standing 33 inches on its plinth, dates back to 1895. It was cast, modelled and engraved by one of the finest Victorian silversmiths. The trophy is elaborately engraved and on the lid is the detailed figure of a footballer from the Victorian age.

There is no accurate record of the first thirty odd years in the history of the trophy, but by 1923 a definite link with football had been established. It was known then as the Viscountess Furness Football Cup and was competed for by teams from a shipbuilding firm called the Furness Withy Company based on Teesside. The trophy would have borne the names of all the different sections of the shipyard who had won the competition, such as the Platers Helpers in 1923.

The story of the trophy before 1923 remains a mystery although the Furness Withy Company had been in operation since 1893, when Christopher Furness took over the shipbuilding yard of Edward Withy.

The Viscountess Furness Football Cup survived right up until 1968 when it was won by a team from the Haverton Hills

Shipyard. Sadly, the side from Haverton Hills was split up in 1969 when their yard was closed down. It wasn't until April 1987 that the team were re-united by Littlewoods and invited to Wembley as their guests for the Liverpool v Arsenal final. Amongst the players present was their skipper Les Crank, who had played for Brian Clough at Darlington.

The whereabouts of the trophy between 1968 and 1985 when Littlewoods found the cup are also a mystery. Its condition suggested it had been locked away somewhere and left to tarnish. Littlewoods, however, could see that it really was a beautiful trophy and so they restored it to its former glory.

By the time Kenny Sansom picked up the cup from Sir John Moores — President of the Littlewoods Organisation — it was a very suitable trophy for the League's premier knock-out competition. And now, thanks to Charlies Nicholas's two goals, it has pride of place in the Highbury trophy cabinet.

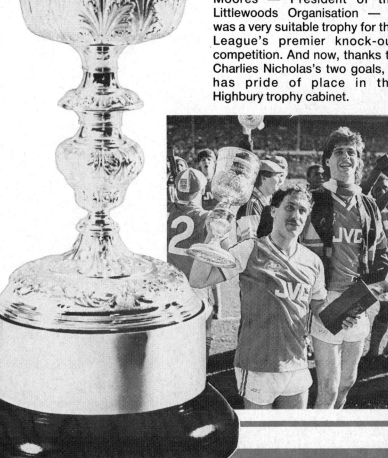

87

# DREAM DOUBLE –

## That's the achievement of Wales and Everton captain KEVIN RATCLIFFE.

Captain of the First Division Champions; captain of my country; you could hardly imagine anything that would give a professional footballer more cause for pride than that double.

I'd always dreamed of playing for Everton. Hoped, too, one day to pull on a Wales shirt. To skipper both sides is beyond my wildest dreams.

The fact I was leading out both club and country at the age of 23 made the honours even more pleasing. It's not very common for a player of that age to hold down even one of the jobs.

I don't know if there's something in my make-up that persuades a manager like Howard Kendall at Everton and

△ **Pat Van Den Hauwe**

◁ **KEVIN RATCLIFFE**

Wales chief Mike England to hand me the captain's armband. You would have to ask them. But I love the responsibility of leadership and I don't feel it has affected my game adversely, as happens with some players.

When I first took over the job for Wales, for instance, we'd had a succession of seven or eight skippers, most of whom hardly played international football again after being captain.

It seemed to spell the start of bad patches for many of them, and sometimes the pressure does affect you.

I must admit, I wasn't playing particularly well for Wales at the time I was given the job. It has been only in the last year or so that I've felt my international form has matched the standards I know I'm capable of.

But I believe that was mainly down to the fact I had no regular recognised centre-half playing alongside me. My partners kept on changing, and many of them were players not really suited to the position.

At that time, the squad wasn't as strong as it is today. We had to move people about to field a side. And that didn't help players to hit it off with team-mates.

But then we got a lucky break with the revelation that my Goodison Park team-mate Pat Van Den Hauwe was eligible to play for any of the home countries since he had become a British citizen after his move from Belgium.

England were immediately after him as cover for established left back Kenny Sansom. But I suppose having Neville Southall and I ear-bashing him about the merits of playing for Wales was a big factor in the decision Pat eventually made.

We told him he shouldn't think of choosing England. Sansom was such a strong and obvious first choice Pat would hardly get a look in. They would probably play him once then forget his name!

Of course, we in the Welsh party needed all the good players we could get. Pat was a particularly valuable acquisition as he could play both at left back and in the centre of defence.

Pat has played most of his games for Wales alongside me at centre-half. And having a partner like him has undoubtedly improved my own form at international level.

We now possess the strongest squad we have had for many years. We used to struggle badly if we had one or two injuries, but now we seem to be able to cope with the loss of even our best players because there is competition for places.

I've been particularly impressed with the younger players who have been forcing their way into the reckoning. Men such as Malcolm Allen of Watford, Andy Jones of Port Vale and Neil Slatter of Oxford United.

They have a lot of ability and have already shown in squad get-togethers they have the right temperament. We older lads have to knock them down a little just to keep them in their place!

The future for Welsh football looks bright with the current combination of experienced men and youngsters. But we could now do with qualifying for either the European Championship Finals or the World Cup Finals to emphasise the quality of the players we have.

We keep missing out by a whisker. Perhaps by a single point or on goal difference. As a result, some of the world class players we have, such as Ian Rush and Neville Southall, have never been given the chance to perform against the best.

I'll always remember watching the World Cup in Mexico and feeling so envious of the England, Scotland and Northern Ireland players who had the opportunity of showing how they could compete on football's biggest stage.

People have said to me that I was very close to being eligible to play for England. I was born in Mancot, close to the English border near Chester. I'm a Welshman by about three miles!

But three miles is a long way. Especially when your mum and dad and your grandparents are Welsh. I don't have a drop of English blood in me and could never consider playing for anyone but Wales.

North Wales football has taken a terrific leap forward in recent years. It has become even more of a hot-bed of talent than some of the more traditional player-producing regions of the country.

Myself, Neville Southall, Ian Rush and Mark Hughes are all from that part of the world. So, too, are Andy Jones and Tony Norman, the Hull goalkeeper.

When I was young there wasn't even a local league to play in. We had to be members of a Chester League. Now there are loads of Sunday Leagues and the number of clubs is above the 50 mark.

I'd like to think there has been a rub-off in terms of interest from what Ian, Neville, Mark and myself have achieved.

It's a joy to skipper such players. But, then, I can honestly say neither the Welsh boys nor the lads at Everton have ever given me any difficulties in terms of discipline on the field.

There are times, of course, when I have to hand out a bit of stick and perhaps have a verbal 'go' at a team-mate. But I'm not exempt from that either if I've made a mistake. You have to be professional enough to give and take criticism.

That applies at either international or club level. I wouldn't lay off someone on Welsh duty just because he is a senior player with another club.

About the only real difference between the two captain posts is that at Everton I'm more involved off-the-field setting up visits from players to hospitals, schools, presentations and so on. That apart, the responsibilities are similar.

But both Wales and Everton have players who will shoulder responsibility themselves. They don't need me telling them what to do all the time.

And if either manager wants to put over a point, he won't necessarily do it through me. He can tell the particular player involved and be sure he will sort it out himself.

As far as I'm concerned captaincy of the two teams I've always aimed at playing for is the icing on the cake.

DAVID LANGAN
*Oxford United*

90

# POWER PLAY

Everton's PAUL POWER sends MIKE DUXBURY (Manchester United) crashing to the ground as he stops a determined challenge.

## FRED STREET looks back on the lighter side of his duties as England "physio".

⚽ I've spent over 150 international matches treating injured England players. But the one that stands out most in my mind is the match when I needed treatment myself! It was a World Cup qualifying game in Oslo in 1981. A vital match in the build-up towards the finals in Spain.

The dressing room before the kick-off was the usual hive of activity. Players bending and stretching, getting changed, asking for treatment or strapping. It was a little cramped for space as I knelt down strapping a player's ankle.

Behind me, goalkeeper Ray Clemence was going through his warming-up routine. He concentrates on a series of exercises to warm up the upper part of his body.

I completed my task on the ankle and stood up — just as Ray was swinging his arms round. Ray caught me on the back of the head and knocked me for six across the dressing room! I was out cold for a few seconds.

Of course all the lads fell about laughing. It really eased the tension in the dressing room. Perhaps too much because they went out and lost the match 2-1!

Massaging legs . . . strapping ankles . . . a trainer's job doesn't just involve treating injuries. The strangest task I ever had as England physio was to stretch Terry Butcher's shirts and Peter Shilton's jerseys!

Before the present outfitters, Umbro, took over, the suppliers of the England kit always delivered standard size shirts. At 6 ft. 4 in. tall and with a big chest, Terry couldn't get into the biggest shirt available until I spent time pulling and stretching it in the dressing room.

The same with the goalkeeping jersey. Peter Shilton has very long arms, perhaps one of the secrets of his ability between the posts. The standard sized jersey finished halfway up his arms — until I did the stretching job.

Nowadays big Terry and Shilts can play in comfort. Umbro supply 'tailor-made' kit for England — an extra-large size shirt for Terry Butcher and jerseys with extra-long sleeves for Peter Shilton.

Fellow physio Norman Medhurst, of Chelsea, and I are the 'baggage men' on international trips. We take charge of all the kit, as well as all our own equipment and supplies.

It's a major operation for an event like the World Cup. When we went out to Mexico for the finals, Norman and I were in charge of 174 pieces of baggage!

They included more than 20 sets of first choice playing strip for each of the 22 players — over 450 England shirts! For every international match, two shirts are provided. One for each player to keep and one to swap with the opposition.

For the World Cup we also took five sets of training kit for

**RAY CLEMENCE** ▶

**FRED STREET** ▼

# BY RAY CLEMENCE!

each player. Three or four pairs of boots each. Plus track suits, towels and other bits and pieces. It took months to set it all up. Norman and I tend to estimate highly what we'll need — and then add a bit!

We have to work out how

many ankle strappings we'll need. We normally work on the basis of three dozen for a three day trip involving one international. You can imagine how many ankle strappings went with us to Mexico!

Then there are bandages, plasters, sprays and creams and things like sun-tan oil for places such as Mexico where the lads want to get a bit of sun.

Then there are studs and laces for the boots, inner soles, pads and all kinds of things. And, for the World Cup, about 50 footballs that have to be pumped up on arrival.

On most trips Norman and I are given an extra hotel room which is stripped bare and we set up our headquarters. It's a bit like a supermarket once we have everything organised because

often we take certain items of food that may be difficult to get abroad.

Footballers are very fussy types. They like going away but still like to feel as if they are at home. They love their cornflakes for breakfast. Their H.P. sauce with main meals. It's surprising how hard it is to find orange squash in many countries. Mostly it's either pure orange or a fizzy drink. So we take a few bottles of orange squash that can be diluted with bottled mineral water.

Milk chocolate is another special demand. The lads don't like most of the chocolate you get abroad, so we always have a few bars of milk chocolate. A lot of players like rice pudding as a pre-match meal, so there are always a few tins of that in the baggage.

We also include lots of team photos, F.A. badges and other little things to dish out to local fans. It helps to make friends which can be a help when you are a long way from home.

The funniest moment I can recall in connection with the England baggage happened when we were on our way to the World Cup in Mexico.

We had been preparing in Canada for the finals, and were flying out from Los Angeles in an Air Mexico jet after breaking the journey from Vancouver.

It was chaotic at the airport because when we turned up for the flight we found we were not registered. We were a large party, but seats were found for us all in the end. However, just as we were about to take off, I looked out of the window and saw half of our baggage still sitting on the tarmac!

An American passenger had also spotted his case left behind, and demanded the take-off be halted.

"If my bag's not going, I'm not going!" he shouted.

After an hour's delay all our bags were loaded, but the problems still were not over. The

aircraft was so heavily laden it had to make an unscheduled stop at the little Mexican airport of Chihuahua to re-fuel on the way to Monterrey.

Security is always very tight these days on international trips. This was very much the case during the 1982 World Cup in Spain. There were armed guards all round our hotels.

It was a new thing for Norman and myself to be assigned our own personal bodyguards. We always went down to the ground ahead of the players to lay out all the strips and prepare the dressing room.

Our armed guards came everywhere with us. We got to know them well and ended up nicknaming them 'Starsky and Hutch'.

In Mexico we found ourselves facing the guns ourselves on one worrying occasion. We were due to train one day at the Aztec Stadium, but found we were barred from using it for some reason. So we went over to the Atlantic Stadium where we had trained once before — only to find it padlocked. Despite loud knocking at the gates nobody came to let us in — until our driver snapped the lock off.

Then we were surrounded by officials and police and trigger-happy troops. It was all a little nerve-racking until things were smoothed over and we could get on with the job of training for our World Cup quarter-final.

Now, of course, I'm looking forward to the next European Championship finals in West Germany, and beyond that to the 1990 World Cup in Italy.

The last time I went with England to the European finals in 1980, it was held in Italy. And one of my tasks in our first match against Belgium was to treat the players for the effects of tear-gas in their eyes after police fired canisters into the rioting fans.

Next time I'd like to concentrate on the football injuries — and hopefully not too many of those.

# DOUBLE INJURY BLOW

## BUT MY DREAM STILL CAME TRUE!

### Celtic's ANTON ROGAN explains why.

⚽ I reckon Celtic took a big risk in signing me and I'm delighted I've been able to repay the club's faith in my ability by graduating to the first team and hanging on to my place.

But why the risk? Well, the truth is that, from the time Celtic first showed an interest in me until I actually signed, I managed to break my leg not once, but twice!

That was while I was playing in the Irish League for Belfast side Distillery. Although I was only 17 I'd managed to attract interest from a number of clubs.

Chelsea, Queen's Park Rangers and Leicester all fancied me. I'd also had a two week trial with Arsenal, but I found the London club wasn't really my scene.

You see, it was in the back of my mind that Celtic were showing an interest and it had been my dream to play for the famous Glasgow club.

I'd always been a Celtic fanatic and regularly travelled to Parkhead with my local Celtic supporters' club from Andersontown.

But, just when Celtic seemed set to sign me, disaster struck. The date — 13th October, 1984 — is still etched in my memory. In a league match I broke my leg for the first time. To my horror, I discovered Celtic had been set to sign me the following week in a £30,000 deal. I was shattered.

As far as I was concerned, my chance of joining the Glasgow club had gone. Who'd want a

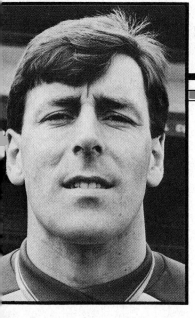

youngster with a broken leg? But, to my surprise, Celtic chief scout John Kelman kept in touch with me, checking on my recovery.

As it happened I was back in action quickly — probably too quickly. I was able to play in the Distillery team just after Christmas and stayed there until the end of the season.

It was then Celtic came back for me. I was invited to play for their under-20 side in an international tournament in Holland.

It was my big chance to show that I'd recovered from injury, and against top class continental opposition at that. But again my luck was out. Playing against the East German national team I broke the same leg again!

The strange thing is that on both occasions when I broke my leg I was playing out of position in the sweeper's role. So that's a position I'm pretty superstitious about now!

After my second leg-break, I thought my career was at an end. I couldn't see how any professional club would take an interest in a young player who'd broken the same leg twice in under a year.

The doctors reckoned I'd come back from the first break too quickly and that I hadn't given the leg enough time to heal.

This time I was in plaster for two months. I knew if I was to

have any chance of making a successful return I couldn't rush back too quickly.

So, during the day, I helped out on the Distillery groundstaff. And, whenever I could, I journeyed over to Glasgow to see Celtic.

It was February before I started playing again. Although Celtic had kept in touch, I couldn't see any chance of them coming back for me a third time.

So, I was as surprised as anyone when Celtic invited me over during the summer of last year. But, unfortunately, there was a transfer wrangle that I feared might put the deal off.

Distillery wanted the £30,000 Celtic had offered for me two years previously. Quite naturally, Celtic pointed out that, as I'd broken my leg twice since then, my value had dropped considerably. And I agreed with Celtic. They were taking a big risk in signing me. Eventually it was resolved and I joined for under £10,000.

Once I signed, I set my sights on winning a first-team place. But I wondered if I'd ever get a chance in the top side.

There was a lot of talk about the manager signing big-name defenders to boost the first-team squad. The likes of Chelsea's Joe McLaughlin and Steve Clarke — then with St Mirren — and Norwich City star Steve Bruce were all mentioned as possible Celtic recruits.

If one or more of them had signed it would obviously have made it even more difficult for me to force my way into the team.

But, as luck would have it, none of those deals came off, and I was fortunate enough to get my chance after we'd suffered a bad defeat at the hands of Old Firm rivals Rangers on New Year's Day.

I made my debut just 48 hours later when we met Hamilton Accies at Parkhead. I

thought I'd be very nervous. But, once the game started, I just got on with it like everyone else.

It's easy to settle in when there are experienced players like Roy Aitken and Pat Bonner alongside you, constantly offering advice and always there to help if you're in trouble.

Then the fact I scored the only goal of our match against Hibs in only my third first-team game obviously did a lot to help me settle down.

So far, I must say I've been surprised at how well I've done. But I've just been concentrating on not making any mistakes and trying to help our attacks whenever I can.

At the moment, my main ambition is simply to try to keep my place in the side, and hopefully do well enough to have a long career with Celtic. Naturally, I'm keen to get in amongst the medals as I've never won anything in football.

My home in Belfast is full of medals and trophies that I've won playing Gaelic Football, and I'd love to add some soccer honours to my collection.

I love playing Gaelic Football, though obviously I can't play any more due to my Celtic commitments. It's such a tough game. I think it's done a lot to develop my stamina and fitness, and it's certainly helped me to develop more quickly as a footballer.

Something else that's pleased me is how well I've been treated by the Celtic supporters. Already I've had two supporters' clubs named after me.

One is in Glasgow's Penilee district, while the other, surprisingly, is a newly-formed club in Southampton.

They've named their club the Rogan-Roache Celtic Supporters' Club after me and my club-mate from Dublin, Declan Roache.

Let's hope I can give them plenty to cheer about!

**IAN CROOK**
*Norwich City*

96

**IAN RUSH**
*Juventus*

97

# NO LET-UP AT LOFTUS ROAD

⚽ September the 1st 1981 was a significant date for football. Queen's Park Rangers played Luton Town at Loftus Road in the first Football League match on an artificial pitch.

Q.P.R.'s Chairman Jim Gregory had gone ahead and had a plastic pitch laid despite the reservations of bodies such as the Football Association and Football League.

Perhaps the best advertisement for the new surface was provided by Luton Town that very first night. They showed such a liking for the pitch, they beat Rangers 2-1, thereby proving that the surface was not an overwhelming advantage to the home side.

In fact, Luton developed such a taste for plastic that four years later they became the second club to lay an artificial pitch, to be followed a year later by Oldham Athletic and Preston North End. Now, of course, the F.A. have tried to halt the trend by banning the playing of F.A. Cup ties on artificial pitches.

But for many clubs, plastic pitches are seen as a financial life-line. The surface may not be tops for soccer, but it's perfect for a range of other activities — and can be rented out.

A plastic pitch can be used for 24 hours a day without wear and tear. Boards can be put down and then seating erected over it so that no damage is done to the surface.

## QUEENS PARK RANGERS' PLASTIC PITCH IS ALWAYS IN DEMAND

It is not affected by frost, and snow can be easily swept off. Rain goes straight through it.

In short, an artificial pitch turns a football stadium into a centre that can be used every minute, every day of the year — instead of a liability that is in full use on average only once every two weeks.

Queen's Park Rangers have made the most of their plastic pitch. Rarely a day goes by without some kind of activity at Loftus Road. Four days a week the ground is hired out afternoon and evening, to company teams or clubs playing in local leagues. Most dates are booked — at a charge of £250 plus VAT. Floodlights for evening games cost another £180.

Earlier this year a film company took over the ground for three days and nights to make a commercial for an airline. The ground was re-marked out as an American grid-iron pitch, and filming went on day and night.

Barry McGuigan won his World Featherweight title at Loftus Road. A purpose-built boxing ring in the centre of the pitch gave McGuigan the chance to attract thousands of spectators to roar him to victor over Eusebio Pedrosa.

The evangelical preacher Luis Palau had a six-week long 'season' one summer at the Rangers stadium.

Rangers have staged international hockey matches five-a-side rugby tournaments international lacrosse matches cannon-ball cricket leagues; and American football. There have been pop concerts, Sunday morning markets and demonstration short-tennis games.

The marketing success of the artificial pitch has persuaded Queen's Park Rangers to consider further ways of developing the ground. They have plans in the pipeline for a retractable roof over the pitch to protect players and spectators from the weather.

Now they are discussing the practicalities of a retractable floor — just in case they decide to go back to a grass pitch and still want to stage other events.

"I don't think we've yet made full use of the facilities we have available at Loftus Road," says commercial manager Brian Rowe. "We are constantly investigating new ways of making use of our ground for other events."

Laying a plastic pitch revolutionised Queen's Park Rangers. The game will never be the same again — even if everyone does prefer grass for football.

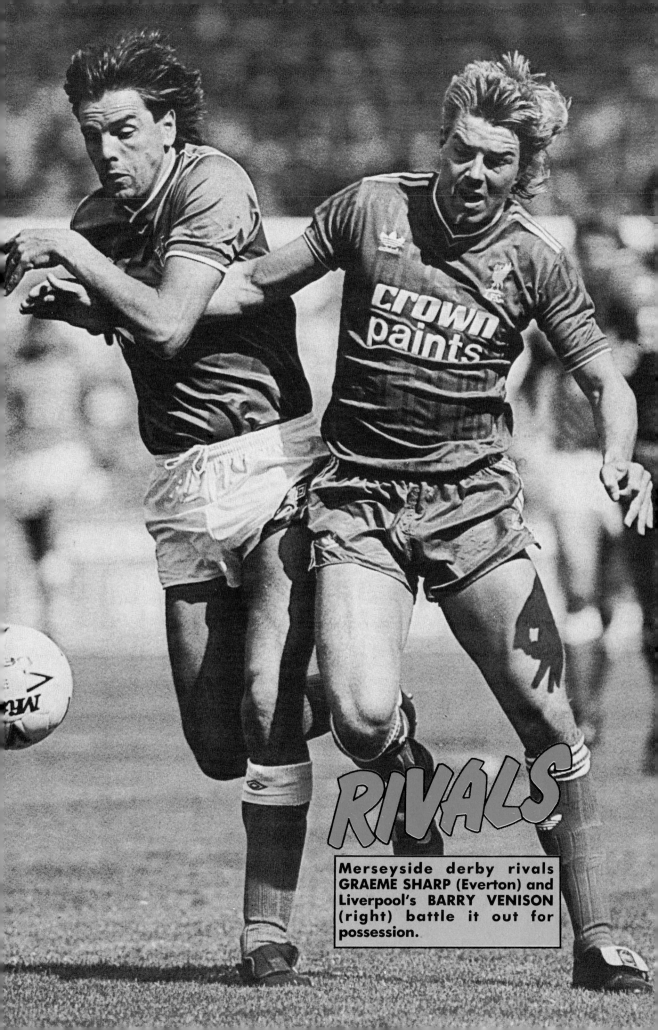

# RIVALS

Merseyside derby rivals GRAEME SHARP (Everton) and Liverpool's BARRY VENISON (right) battle it out for possession.

# CROSSWORD

## ACROSS

1. Meaty part of London club (3)
3. Goal scorer Gary (7)
6. Kevin of the Reds (5)
7. Alloa's nickname (5)
8. Desperate managers often . . . the changes (4)
9. A good defender does this to his lines (6)
12. West Ham's number one (6)
14. Clive and Paul of Spurs (5)
16. Chelsea's Scottish striker (5)
17. Merseyside marvels (7)

## DOWN

1. Referees are sometimes accused of being one (5)
2. Pompey striker (7)
3. Goes with goal or bye (4)
4. Luton striker (6)
5. Cautious teams don't take these (5)
10. Scotland's "Diamonds" (7)
11. Goes with Oxford's Saunders (6)
12. A first team one is every player's aim (5)
13. Good keepers must be this (5)
15. Q.P.R.'s Sammy (3)
16. Millwall feel at home here (3)

*See 3 Across* ▷

*Answers on page 124*

TIM BREAKER
Luton Town

101

# UNWANTED!

## That was the shock news that sent MARK FALCO on his way to Watford.

IT came as a shock to me last season when I realised I wasn't wanted any longer at Tottenham. After nine years at White Hart Lane, the last two of them as the club's leading goal scorer, the news of a move came out of the blue.

But once I got over the first shock, I came to terms with the idea. If you don't fit in at one club you have to go to a team that does want you.

I went into training one day at Tottenham and was told that Watford wanted to sign me. The more I thought about it, the better it looked for me, but it was still a huge decision to actually leave Spurs after so many years.

It wasn't until later in the season that I finally knew I'd made the right move — when I turned up for training at Watford and found only half the first team players there!

You see, during my time with Spurs I got used to being one of the few first team players around the club during international weeks.

Most of the side were often away playing for their country. Men like Ray Clemence, Glenn Hoddle, Chris Waddle, Clive Allen, Gary Mabbutt, Gary Stevens and Graham Roberts with England, Chris Hughton and Tony Galvin with the Republic of Ireland, Steve Archibald and Alan Brazil (Scotland), Paul Price (Wales) and other players at Under-21 level. I'd be virtually on my own as a first teamer, left to train with the reserves or youth team.

Obviously I was a little envious. I always wished L was off playing for England myself. But I got used to it, and nobody at White Hart Lane looked down on me because I wasn't an international player. Every player is treated the same there, as they are at Watford.

I expected it to be a lot different at Vicarage Road. I thought there would be only the odd player away on international duty.

Then one week Watford had centre-half John McClelland away with Northern Ireland,

Kenny Jackett and Malcolm Allen (Wales), John Barnes with England, and two youngsters, full-back Nigel Gibbs, and midfield man Gary Porter in the England Under-21 squad. It brought home to me that Watford are a club with their own star players, and a lot of potential in the younger lads.

There's another point. All those players are skilful footballers. I think it destroyed the idea that Watford are just a crash-bang-wallop team. The side gained that reputation unjustly when first promoted to the First Division, because their style relied a lot on the long ball.

But, in the last year or two, things have changed. At Watford we play as much thoughtful football as anyone. We have players with genuine skills.

I have settled in well, and there are certainly no regrets from me about leaving Tottenham. Of course I have plenty of memories from my Spurs days — happy ones mostly.

I'll never forget the night we won the UEFA Cup at White Hart Lane. It all came down to penalties at the end of the second leg, after two 1-1 draws

with the crack Belgian side Anderlecht. Before the game we'd sorted out who would take any penalties, never really thinking we'd be called into action.

But as the final whistle blew after extra time had failed to produce a winning goal, I remember we all looked at each other, thinking 'this is it'. Some players couldn't bear to watch the kicks being taken. But I watched every one.

Graham Roberts took the first one and scored. Steve Archibald put away the second. And when goalkeepr Tony Parks saved from Morten Olsen, it meant we were ahead 2-1.

Then it was my turn. I took a deep breath, ran up and drove the ball home. What a relief.

The Belgians pulled one back to 3-2, Gary Stevens made it 4-2, and then it was 4-3. Danny Thomas had the chance to clinch the cup for Spurs with our final penalty but his shot was saved.

The Belgians could still equalise with their last shot. But Tony Parks made himself the hero of the night with a brilliant save from Icelandic star Arnor Gudjohnsen.

It was a fantastic night of

**MATCHWINNER — the penalty save by Tony Parks that won Spurs the UEFA Cup.**

celebration at White Hart Lane, especially for me. It was my first medal with Spurs, having missed out on two F.A. Cup wins. Three times Spurs have been at Wembley in the last six years for the F.A. Cup Final, and once for the Milk Cup — and I missed them all.

Last season Spurs earned their Wembley place by beating Watford in the semi-final — and that has got to be one of the biggest disappointments of my life. It was no consolation to lose to my old club. In fact it was worse for me to get so close to Wembley with Watford, but see my old mates beat us.

But I do have one outstanding Wembley memory. My first big match for Spurs was the 1981 Charity Shield game against Aston Villa, when I replaced the injured Garth Crooks in the Cup-winning side.

It was a great occasion for me. For some reason I felt no nerves walking out at Wembley for the first time. I managed to hit two good goals to help us draw 2-2.

Those two goals set me off on a good scoring run. I hit nine in the first eleven games of the season, and I was playing well. Then I suffered a bad ankle injury, and that really set me back. Although I was playing again in a few months, it took me 18 months to fully recover.

The injury cost me a chance of playing in the F.A. Cup Final in 1982, and I did let myself get 'down'. I found myself relegated to about fifth choice at Spurs, and it was hard to get motivated.

The low point of my career came when I was loaned to Chelsea, who were then in the Second Division. I played three matches for them, and the plan was that if I did well they might make the move permanent.

Perhaps that was the reason why I couldn't seem to kick a ball right for Chelsea. Nothing went well for me at Stamford Bridge, and after a month they sent me back to Tottenham.

The experience made me realise I had to get down to some hard work, and sharpen myself up, if I was going to regain a first team place at Spurs.

I went to an athletics coach to help me speed up my movement and reflexes, and when I got another chance in the side I was a different player. After that I hardly looked back, and it was only the arrival of David Pleat as manager, with his own ideas on team selection, that ended a good run in the team.

Around the time that I was a

MARK FALCO

bit low in confidence, Spurs were using two sports psychologists to try to get the best out of the players.

The psychologists taught me to think positively about scoring goals, rather than be negative and worry about the missed chances. Thinking positively, for me, however, does not mean setting goalscoring targets. I've

never done that. I think it can be harmful.

I feel that if you set yourself a specific goal target you can spend too much time trying to reach it, and ignore the needs of the team. It can make you selfish.

I feel I am a team player. I don't see myself purely as a goalscorer. If I can lay on a goal or a chance for a colleague I'm doing my job just as much as if

I'm scoring goals myself.

I like to score goals — but the match result is what matters. I'm happy if my team wins, whether I score or not. These days that team is Watford, and I'm looking foward to the next few years at Vicarage Road.

I believe we have the set-up and the players to be very successful in the future.

STEVE BAKER
*Southampton*

104

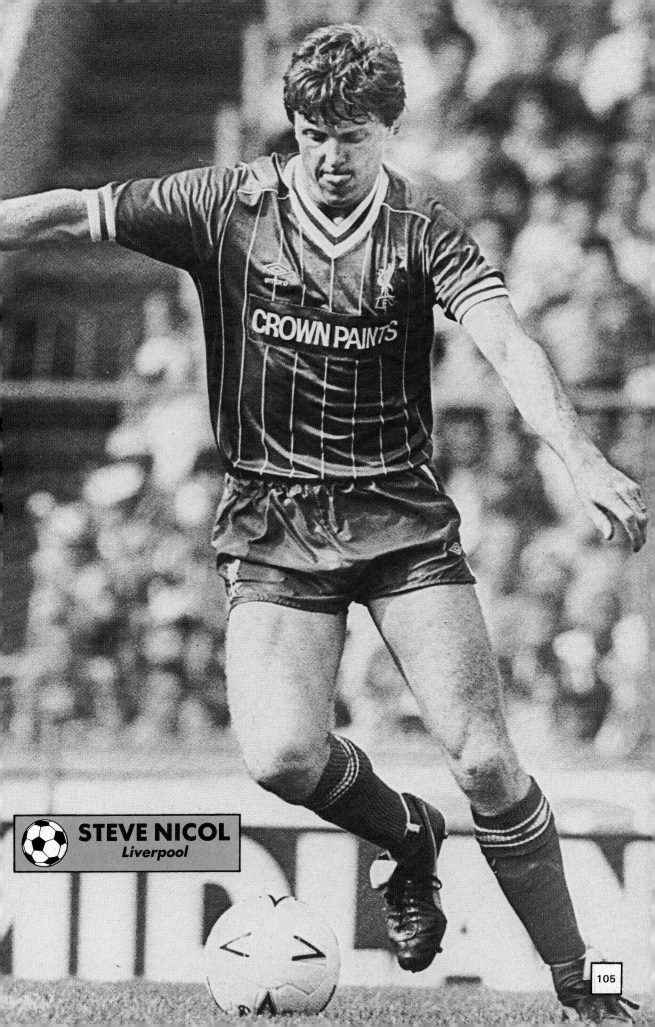

STEVE NICOL
*Liverpool*

105

⚽ Four years ago Sheffield Wednesday's Martin Hodge went on one of the regular 'extras' in most footballers' schedules — a visit to a local hospital.

The Hillsborough goalkeeper, like the bulk of his fellow professionals, had done many such 'perk 'em up' trips to children and adult wards in the past.

This particular afternoon visit, however, so affected Martin that he began a fund at Wednesday which snowballed well beyond expectations.

"We were being shown around wards in a children's hospital. There was a baby boy there who was only six months old and he'd been diagnosed as having leukaemia," Martin recalls.

"I couldn't believe it. I was terribly shocked. When you have children of your own who are fit and healthy, something like that really hits home.

"My team-mate at the time, Mick Lyons, now manager at Grimsby, was also numbed by the experience. He, too, had a healthy young family.

"Both of us came away from the hospital thinking how fortunate we were to be physically and mentally fit and enjoying the outdoor life of sportsmen.

"We knew that, as footballers and thus very much in the spotlight, our efforts might

# HELPING HANDS AT HILLSBOROUGH

## HOW SHEFFIELD WEDNESDAY'S *MARTIN HODGE* AND HIS TEAM-MATES ARE DOING THEIR BEST FOR CHILDREN IN NEED

generate more interest than some. We were not in it for personal glory, but we realised we had a better chance than most to do something about raising money.

"Mick and I decided to set up the Sheffield Wednesday players' children's fund."

Functions and presentations were already being attended regularly — very often four or five times a week — by Wednesday's first-team squad. A small fee for petrol expenses was in most cases the only expenditure for the folk wanting their services. More often than not these public relations exercises were being done free of charge.

Hodge realised this was a major avenue for cash that Wednesday could tap to boost their fund.

"As we were giving up plenty of time anyway to attend special functions and prize-givings, it seemed logical to ask if a small donation could be made to the fund," says Martin.

"Folk were happy to oblige. Basically that is how I reckoned we could do our small part to raising money for the kids.

"Then other things started creeping into the fund-raising. We would take along autographed footballs and Wednesday shirts and auction them off.

"Word began to get around and soon we were being asked to attend sponsored walks and fun runs. My mail at the club became astronomical. Fans were sending me money that they had collected at their own fund-raising events.

"Youngsters were giving me their pocket money and cash they'd received from jumble sales in their back gardens!

"There was an absolutely tremendous response. In one year we raised £8000, some of which went towards refurbishing a centre for the handicapped in Sheffield."

Big firms chipped in with their help. A holiday company offered a break for two in Scotland as a raffle prize and a garage donated £800 worth of toys to be distributed around hospitals at Christmas.

"Every visit to the wards makes the whole venture worthwhile," Martin goes on.

"I organise which of the team do which visits. We usually go in threes and I make sure we go as a whole squad on at least three occasions in a year.

"It is touching to realise how much our visits help. Strikers Lee Chapman and Brian Marwood went to see a young boy at his home who was in a full plaster up to his waist after several operations.

"His mum wrote to thank us and said he'd never stopped talking about Lee and Brian's visit ever since he met them.

"The highlight for me, however, was when the club organised a Sportacular at Hillsborough and parks in the Sheffield area.

"It is run every school half term and the kids come along and have three days' entertainment. It was decided to extend the event to the handicapped.

"Blind and wheel-chair bound kids were invited and all they wanted to do was play the first team at football. We split into two groups in the gym and those games turned out to be the toughest matches we played all season!

"We played the blind youngsters using a ball with a bell inside. To watch them locating the ball and lining themselves up to strike it properly was amazing.

"The bell was barely audible, yet their hearing was so sensitive they could pick up the sound incredibly accurately. We played the last few minutes with our eyes shut, and you've no idea how frightening that was!

"In the match against the handicapped boys we played on our hands and knees and they were bashing us about and running us over with their wheelchairs!

"You can win all sorts of medals and trophies in this game, but the satisfaction we gained that day was something I'll never forget. I'm just glad I am in a position to help out in some way."

**JOHN BAILEY**
Newcastle United

108

# Close your eyes – and hope for the best!

That seems to be the approach favoured by both Luton's ROBERT WILSON (left) and JOHN MILLAR (Chelsea) as they challenge for a cross ball.

## That's tough talking from West Ham's pint-sized midfielder MARK WARD.

⚽ A good big'un will always beat a good little'un. That's what they say — but I hope to be the one to smash that theory. At 5ft 6 ins tall I'm one of the smallest players in the First Division, but I still have ambitions to be one of the best.

Being small hasn't held back my West Ham colleague Tony Cottee. He's played for England and is one of the most consistent goalscorers in the game. Although Tony is an inch or two taller than me, people often confuse us, as I found to my cost last year!

We were playing a pre-season friendly match, and early in the game, Tony was booked for a tackle. The ref told him 'any more of that and you're off'. A few minutes later I was pulled up for a foul. It was my first offence of the game, yet I was sent off!

To this day I'm convinced the referee mistook me for Tony. In fact Tony tried to tell the official he'd got the wrong man, but it did no good.

Quite often, too, fans have asked me to 'sign your autograph, Tony', and on occasion even West Ham directors have confused the two of us.

I just wish that England manager Bobby Robson would make the same mistake! I'd love to get into the England squad — but the nearest I've been is when a national newspaper printed my picture instead of Tony Cottee's to announce his selection for the squad.

Of course I still hope to impress Mr Robson in my own right. I've got a long way to go, of course, but as I say — small is beautiful.

I was even smaller than I am now, when I had my first contact with professional football — as a ball-boy at Everton. I had always been an Everton fan, and when I was old enough I signed schoolboy forms. When I heard the club wanted ball-boys, I jumped at the chance to get so close to my favourite players.

The stars of the Everton side in those days were Bob Latchford, the big centre-forward, midfielder Andy King, and winger Dave Thomas. It was a great chance for me to get a good look at how they played.

Another ball-boy at the same time was Steve McMahon who went on to play for Everton before going to Aston Villa, and then on to Liverpool.

Steve was just over a year older than me and he got a full contract as a professional with the club. But when I was old enough to become a fully-fledged professional footballer, the club showed me the door and my dreams of a career in the game seemed over.

I was surprised and disappointed that they didn't keep me on. But at that time Everton weren't in such a strong position financially as they are now. The team was very much in the shadow of neighbours Liverpool, and never came close to winning anything. That meant that there were restrictions on the number of players they could have on the staff.

So, along with five or six others, I was told that there was no future for me at the club. Two players who did manage to get contracts at that time were Gary Stevens, who went on to play at full-back for England and Kevin Richardson, who now plays for Watford. But I was destined for the dole queue.

At first during that summer I hoped that another League club might give me the chance to prove Everton wrong. But it was non-League side Northwich Victoria who stepped in with the first offer. It wasn't quite what I was hoping for, but at least the money was better than the dole and the football was actually of quite a high standard.

When I joined Northwich I really didn't know anything about non-League football. I had been brought up at one of the biggest clubs in the country and I really couldn't imagine anything different to life at Goodison. But, although it was a shock at first, I soon got used to life with Northwich. In fact, the time I spent there proved to be a very useful experience. And I was even to get a trip to Wembley while I was there.

That was for the F.A. Trophy Final in 1983, a game which turned out to be my last in non-League football. Unusually for me, I'd scored quite a few goals in our Cup run that season, including the winner in the second leg of the semi-final against Dagenham. In the final we were to meet Telford United and we were very hopeful of winning the Cup. But it proved to be a very disappointing day for us, as we didn't play very well and lost 2-1.

It was obviously a great day out for all of us but whatever anybody says, it is still very upsetting to lose at Wembley — even in the F.A. Trophy.

Although I was very down about losing on that May day back in 1983, there was a nice surprise waiting for me because Oldham moved in soon after and signed me up for a return to League football.

By the start of the season, I'd done enough to prove to the manager, Joe Royle, that I was worth a place in the first team. I finally made my debut in League football in a home game against Brighton, who like me, had just experienced defeat at Wembley — against Manchester United in the F.A. Cup Final.

It seemed like I'd been in non-League football for a long time but I was still only twenty

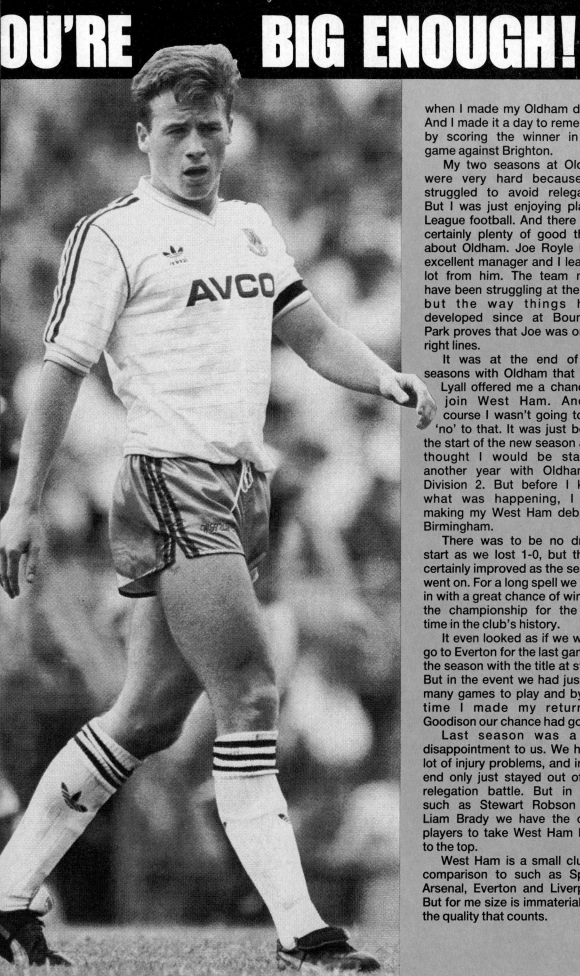

# OU'RE      BIG ENOUGH!

when I made my Oldham debut. And I made it a day to remember by scoring the winner in that game against Brighton.

My two seasons at Oldham were very hard because we struggled to avoid relegation. But I was just enjoying playing League football. And there were certainly plenty of good things about Oldham. Joe Royle is an excellent manager and I learnt a lot from him. The team might have been struggling at the time but the way things have developed since at Boundary Park proves that Joe was on the right lines.

It was at the end of two seasons with Oldham that John Lyall offered me a chance to join West Ham. And of course I wasn't going to say 'no' to that. It was just before the start of the new season and I thought I would be starting another year with Oldham in Division 2. But before I knew what was happening, I was making my West Ham debut at Birmingham.

There was to be no dream start as we lost 1-0, but things certainly improved as the season went on. For a long spell we were in with a great chance of winning the championship for the first time in the club's history.

It even looked as if we would go to Everton for the last game of the season with the title at stake. But in the event we had just too many games to play and by the time I made my return to Goodison our chance had gone.

Last season was a big disappointment to us. We had a lot of injury problems, and in the end only just stayed out of the relegation battle. But in men such as Stewart Robson and Liam Brady we have the class players to take West Ham back to the top.

West Ham is a small club in comparison to such as Spurs, Arsenal, Everton and Liverpool. But for me size is immaterial. It's the quality that counts.

111

TONY COTON
*Watford*

# IT HAPPENED LAST SEASON

1. A player made history by appearing in all four English divisions in the one season. Name him, please.

2. Only one player scored five goals in a Football League match. Who was he?

3. Against which team did Ian Rush score his last goal for Liverpool?

4. Hamilton created the shock of the Scottish Cup by defeating Rangers at Ibrox. Who scored their winning goal?

5. Who were the first club to be officially promoted?

6. Which team won the Full Members Cup?

7. One player was an ever-present in Everton's championship winning side. Name, please.

8. A Scottish Premier Division player hit the headlines by receiving 3 red cards in one game. Name and club, please.

9. Three players were sold to other clubs, but were loaned back to the selling outfit for the rest of the season. Can you name all three?

10. Against which side did Everton clinch the title?

11. Name the player and clubs involved in the most expensive transfer deal of the season.

12. Who was Scotland's leading goalscorer in League games?

13. Clive Allen of Tottenham Hotspur topped the goalscoring charts. What was his over-all total?

14. Only one club scored more than a century of League goals. Who were the club and what was their tally?

15. Which club did Scarborough replace in the Football League?

16. A Scottish goalkeeper set a British record for the longest spell of play without conceding a goal. Name and club, please.

17. Which side were in the top three of their division all season but failed to gain promotion?

18. A player, signed from a non-League outfit, made his only professional appearance in an FA Cup semi-final. Who was he?

19. England manager Bobby Robson gave three players their first full international caps. Name them.

**Answers on Page 124.**

**THERE WERE PLENTY OF MOMENTS TO REMEMBER IN 1986-87. HOW MANY CAN YOU RECALL?**

# MANDIE SIGNS UP THE STARS —BY THE THOUSAND!

Footballers past and present, referees, managers, club officials and journalists are all represented in the thousands of signatures collected by 16-year-old Mandie Nunn during last season.

It was in September 1986, that Mandie decided to capture the signature of every senior footballer playing in season 1986-87.

And if that wasn't a big enough task, Mandie extended her coverage to take in as many people as possible who were involved in football in whatever capacity.

As a result she now has a massive collection which includes such star names as Sir Stanley Matthews, Tom Finney, Bobby Robson, Bobby Charlton, Jimmy Greaves, Bobby Moore — and lots, lots more.

Mandie's collection has raised so much interest that she's been interviewed by newspapers, appeared on television and was a guest of Freight Rover at their Cup Final last May.

It's been a giant undertaking involving writing hundreds of letters and spending a lot of pocket money, but Mandie reckons the response has made all her efforts well worthwhile.

# MARVELLOUS!

That's Rangers and England stalwart **TERRY BUTCHER** talking. Read on to find out why he's so pleased with his first season in Scotland's Premier Division.

⚽ The night I made my debut for Glasgow Rangers convinced me I'd made a terrific career move by venturing north to play in Scotland. The game was a pre-season friendly against Bayern Munich, and more than 36,000 supporters turned up. The atmosphere was incredible.

There was a feeling of passion and excitement that I'd never experienced anywhere else before, even though I'd played in the World Cup Finals with England and a UEFA Cup Final with Ipswich.

The response from the supporters, as I led the team out for the first time, is a memory I'll always cherish.

Supporters have always been important to me throughout my career but even now I am still coming to terms with the amazing level of support that Rangers can command.

At the moment, the players and the fans are reaping the benefits of what has happened to the club under Graeme Souness. And the interest in the club after our successful first season has been phenomenal.

I was quite flattered and overwhelmed at the number of supporters' clubs who named me as their "Player Of The Year". My only regret was that because of the demand it simply hasn't been humanly possible to pick up each award in person. On some

# EVERYTHING'S BUZZIN

nights there'll be as many as eight clubs having their presentations at the same time.

Certainly the last year or so in Scotland with Rangers has convinced me of one thing. This move is the best one I could ever have made. Now, I'd like to finish my career playing for Rangers — providing they'll have me!

There were some people whose eyebrows were raised when I announced I was coming to Scotland, especially as Spurs were also anxious to sign me at the time. But I think everyone has been shown by now that the move has turned out to be a fabulous one for me.

To tell the truth, though, I wasn't really all that concerned about other people's reaction to the move. It was of far more importance to me that I had the total support of my family.

My wife Rita made it plain she'd be prepared to follow me anywhere if it meant furthering my career. And she left me in no doubt how much she'd like to try living in Scotland, if that's what I wanted.

The thing that surprises me is that with the Scottish game enjoying such a boom at the moment, it doesn't make sense that the national team have failed to consistently produce the goods. It certainly isn't down to a shortage of good players in Scotland.

It's often been said that the English First Division is the toughest in the world. Certainly I'd agree that it's one of the best. But I'd like to see a couple of Italian or Brazilian players try their luck in Scotland. Honestly, if you can play in the Premier Division, you can play anywhere in the world! The football's fast and furious and incredibly competitive. All in all, it makes for a very tough league.

I'd love to see how foreign players would cope. They certainly wouldn't be given the same time on the ball they're accustomed to. Premier Division football is certainly not for the faint-hearted.

**GRAEME SOUNESS — plenty to be pleased about.**

One thing, though, I'd advise anyone intent on coming to Scotland to pack their wellies and a raincoat! Everything that is said about the weather up here is true!

When I came to Rangers, there were people who thought that the move would put me under a great deal of pressure, partly because of the stature of the club. And as early as my first visit to the great Ibrox Stadium I realised what they meant.

My first impressions of the place were a bit strange, I suppose. I arrived at the ground late one evening. It was deserted, not a soul in the place. It was totally different to what I'd experienced in Ipswich. Portman Road had a very homely atmosphere.

Standing in the great hallway at Ibrox for the first time, though, you could feel the great tradition of the place. It was all so imposing.

I trained with the first team squad next day, and was immediately impressed by the club's great support through talking to the hundreds of fans who turned up to watch.

I could sense they knew something big was about to happen, and there was a buzz of anticipation about the place. And that's just the way things have turned out.

To say that's pressure is

wrong in my view. Pressure is what I experienced at Ipswich in my last three years there. Then, we were struggling against relegation, and in effect our future, and that of our families, was at stake. That kind of pressure you can do without!

But aiming to win trophies every season with such a top class side as Rangers — well, if that's pressure then I'll gladly take it any day of the week!

Everything is right about the set-up at Ibrox. The club is ambitious and that will do for me. I have a feeling it's only a matter of time before the team establishes itself again as a force in Europe.

I can remember what the atmosphere was like in the Ipswich dressing-room the year we won the UEFA Cup — it was never quite the same again in later seasons. It's a feeling I can recognise again — now with Rangers.

They are a great bunch of lads at Ibrox and I'm sure that Graeme Souness was pretty pleased with his first year as Rangers' manager.

I knew the gaffer before I joined Rangers, and I have the greatest respect for him and what he is trying to achieve at the club. He's everything in fact that would make me want to play for a manager.

I rate the current Rangers squad as highly as any I've played in. The atmosphere in training is good, and the Liverpool influence is very much to the fore.

If that system has proved to be the best in England and Europe over a number of years, then I've no reason to believe it can't prove to be exactly the same here.

The dressing-room banter between the Scottish and English lads is terrific and we often have six-a-side matches against each other in training. Thankfully, there's Northern Ireland's Jimmy Nicholl to act as a referee, though personally, I don't envy him one little bit.

116

# ROUND IBROX

One important part of the daily life at Ibrox has been the introduction of a Yellow Jersey, an idea Chris Woods and I stole from England squad sessions.

As opposed to the Yellow Jersey worn by the leading rider in the Tour de France, our version is worn by the player having the worst time at the morning training sessions!

Each player in the winning side has a vote and I can reveal that assistant manager Walter Smith, coach Phil Boersma and even the gaffer himself have had to don the Yellow Jersey!

Of course, the only time I've had to wear the least-wanted sweater at Ibrox has been down to the rest of the lads ganging up on their skipper. That's my story anyway, and I'm sticking to it!

Away from Rangers, though, for a moment. One of the best things to happen to me last year was to be asked to captain England at Wembley in our 2-0 win over Yugoslavia in the European Championship. What an experience it turned out to be.

Being at the head of the team as I led them out was fabulous, though I must admit the atmosphere couldn't quite match Ibrox before an 'Old Firm' game between Rangers and Celtic.

And though I've captained Ipswich and Rangers in lots of big games, I'll admit I had more butterflies that night than I'd had before a match in a long time.

Happily, we played well and I was delighted when fans told me afterwards that it was the best match they'd seen at Wembley in years.

All in all, I've had a pretty eventful start to my new career in Scotland and one which has been full of surprises.

My own thoughts that there were going to be a few more 'easier' games than in England were a bit off the mark. I only have to think back to our Scottish Cup exit at the hands of Hamilton and our penalty-kick victory over First Division East Fife in the Skol League Cup to realise that!

Also, I thought that playing each team four times a season at least, would lead to sides knowing each other's games inside out. But that hasn't been the case. Against some sides, it's been like facing a different team each time we've met!

Even Scottish goalkeepers have taken me by surprise! It's a complete myth that Scottish goalies aren't as good as their English counterparts. And though I'd have to say that teammate Chris Woods is the best 'keeper in Scotland at the moment, I've been pleasantly surprised at the standard shown by goalkeepers up here.

On a lighter note, I even attended my first-ever Burns' Suppers. One was at Ibrox, but the other was at Bannockburn! Hardly the best place for an Englishman to be found at that time of year — I'll admit. However, I had great fun at both events and even dared to wear a kilt!

But though my sons, Christopher and Edward have been coming out with the occasional, "Och," or "Aye," I have to admit that Burns's poetry is totally beyond me!

**TOP 'KEEPER — Rangers and England star Chris Woods.**

GLENN ROEDER
Newcastle United

118

**BRYAN ROBSON**
*Manchester United*

# SET FOR

## That's the Stein brothers of Luton Town

**MARK STEIN**

⚽ Take the popular Disney film 'Seven Brides for Seven Brothers', make a slight adjustment to 'Seven Sides' — and you have the football-playing Stein family.

The seven Stein brothers have all played football at some level, with pride of place going to Brian Stein, who has an England cap to his credit. The South African born Steins are football crazy.

Eldest brother Edwin was captain of the General Motors Vauxhall Conference side Barnet who narrowly failed to win a place in the Football League last season, coming second to Scarborough.

But that disappointment was outweighed by the progress made at Luton by younger brother Mark, who developed into one of the most promising strikers in the First Division. In fact Brian and Mark developed into a partnership for Luton that threatened to tear apart some of the best defences in the League.

Says Brian Stein, "It was great for me that Mark came through last season. He did well, even though he struggled to win a place in the side once Mick Harford came back from injury.

"A couple of years ago I thought Mark might not make it at League level. But he's worked hard to make himself stronger so that he can withstand challenges. Mark spent a month on loan with Aldershot, and that made all the difference to him. He got his attitude right.

"He was a bit disappointed at the start of last season when he wasn't picked for Luton's first team. I must admit I thought he

# SUCCESS!

was unlucky not to be in because he'd been our best striker in pre-season matches.

"Mark was a bit unsettled, and went off on loan to try to prove a point. He felt hard done by at not being given a proper opportunity.

"But playing for Aldershot in one match he came up against 6 ft. 5 in. centre-backs trying to kick him up in the air. It made him realise how well off he was at Luton. So when he returned to Kenilworth Road he was determined to make a go of it.

"We had a good spell in the side together. I was playing just behind the front two, and if Mark made a run I could always find him. I know how he plays, he has a good football brain.

"Mark was a bit small and frail at one time. He had the skills but not the strength to succeed as a professional. But in the last two years he's worked very hard on weights and exercises to build himself up. He's very sturdy now.

"In the old days when we were young, all the brothers used to go to youth clubs to play football. Mark was the smallest in the family — so we used to stick him in goal!

"It was disappointing for the family when Barnet just failed to win their league last season, which would have give them a place in the Fourth Division.

"We played Barnet in a pre-season friendly match and they were brilliant against us. I didn't realise that non-League clubs were capable of such a high standard of football.

"We beat them only 3-2 and it was a struggle. My brother Edwin was captain, and played very well.

"It would have been great to have another brother playing in the Football League."

Brian Stein has been a Luton Town regular now for ten years. In that time he's scored over 120 League goals in more than 350 League matches. He had a job in the Civil Service, and was an amateur with Edgware Town, when Luton first spotted him.

"There was no gamble in giving up a job to become a footballer. I wasn't happy as a clerk with the National Health Service and I'd always wanted to be a professional player," he says.

"All of us began playing football in Capetown. Football is the great interest of the black people in South Africa, although there wasn't much organisation while we were there. About 18 years ago, we got the chance to come to Britain and we jumped at it.

"It was great for us. We were able to play organised football for the first time at school in London."

The Steins eventually qualified for British passports — which from a football point of view made them eligible for any of the four home countries. Once Brian had established himself as a regular goalscorer with Luton, it wasn't long before Welsh officials began to take an interest in him.

But he rejected any approaches from Wales, holding out for an invitation from England. He was picked as an 'over-age' player for the Under-21 side, and his senior international breakthrough finally came in 1984, when he was picked along with then Luton team-mate Paul Walsh for England's match against France in Paris.

Mark Stein already has England Youth caps, and may yet go on to emulate Brian as a senior international. At the age of 21 he has time to become as good a player as his brother.

"Mark's great on the ball, and has a good understanding of the game." says Brian. "I'd love Mark to go on to collect a full international cap like me."

The Steins have come a long way from the dusty townships of Capetown. They've worked hard for their success — and they hope there's yet more to come.

BRIAN STEIN

121

# I was the spy

⚽ AT the end of last season I became a football scout. But it wasn't because I was thinking of giving up playing the game. I was in fact doing a favour for my father, Terry Wood, chairman of Scarborough Football Club.

At the time, Scarborough were top of the G. M. Vauxhall Conference League and needed just a few more vital points to secure the title and a place in the Fourth Division of the Football League.

One vital game they had to play was away to Sutton, which is to the south-west of London. Because I didn't live too far from Sutton, I was asked to watch one of their matches and do a bit of homework on their style of play.

I knew what was expected because I'd talked to the Chelsea scouts about the job. So after watching Sutton I was able to give Scarborough a complete run-down on all the players they would face, with a special note on danger men and the set-pieces they employed. I was on the phone a lot to my dad during that period and I'm glad to say that it paid off because Scarborough went on to beat Sutton.

That was a very important result but the championship was actually clinched when Scarborough's nearest challengers, Barnet, lost at home to Stafford. I went to that match and, whenever I could, I rang up dad to let him know what was happening. It wasn't easy to get on the phone that night but when Stafford scored their winner two minutes from time, I made sure I got the news through to everybody at Scarborough.

It was a great moment for dad and the club and everybody came out to celebrate for the last game of the season. There was a crowd of over 5,000 that day which was more than the gate at First Division Charlton. Of course I was playing myself for Chelsea

# in the stand!

Chelsea's
DARREN
WOOD
reveals his
top-secret
mission!

that afternoon but I had a chance to celebrate later on.

The week after they sealed their place in the Fourth Division, Scarborough arranged a match against Wimbledon. The Dons were appropriate opposition as they themselves had come up from non-League football to finish sixth in Division One last season. My dad is very ambitious for Scarborough but I don't think he could even dream of repeating Wimbledon's success. In fact, I'm sure he'd be quite happy at first just to build up a strong base for the club in the lower divisions.

I was delighted when I was asked to appear as a guest for Scarborough. I'd actually played against Wimbledon the night before for Chelsea in a testimonial, but Scarborough gave them a much tougher match. I was happy to share in a victory over Wimbledon, something which I'd failed to do with Chelsea.

It was great for me to share in my dad's glory, especially as he hadn't enjoyed much success as a player himself. He was actually on Leeds' books as a youngster but he was released before being given a real chance.

His connection with Scarborough began when he joined the club to play at non-League level. He had some good years with the club before being forced to retire. He stayed in the town and that is where I was born and brought up. When I

started to take football seriously, I quite often trained with the players at the club but to join a League side I had to move fifty miles up the road to Middlesbrough.

I signed on as an apprentice at Ayresome Park and I was still only 17 when I made my League debut against Southampton. I had no idea at the time that I was near selection but, on the Wednesday before the game, our manager Bobby Murdoch told me that I would be playing as a sweeper.

That was quite a prospect because amongst the opposition were players of the quality of Kevin Keegan, Alan Ball and Mike Channon. I will never forget that game even though we lost 2-0. I didn't play again for several months and by the end of the season the club had been relegated to the Second Division.

But the important thing for me was that I'd made a breakthrough to the first team. I was playing in all sorts of different positions but at least I was in the side. And the next season a man arrived who had a tremendous effect on me as a player.

Malcolm Allison took over when we were bottom of the Second Division and almost immediately got us winning games again. He knows exactly how to motivate players and he certainly picked us up off the ground.

He taught me a lot about the game. Malcolm always said that football was full of ups and downs and you had to learn to accept this. That is something I've always remembered!

I found Malcolm's advice was particularly true when I joined Chelsea because it took me quite a while to settle down. In fact, it wasn't until last season, which was my third at Stamford Bridge, that I fully established myself in the side. I had to get used to the different style of play and then to

a new manager when John Hollins took over from John Neal.

But even last season, when I played in more games than nearly any other Chelsea player, I had to adapt to a positional change. My first two years had been as a full-back but last season I was asked to play in midfield. When I was younger I didn't feel strong enough to play in midfield and thought that it would be easier to stick to full-back. Now I feel more confident in the middle of the park.

Last season wasn't an easy one for Chelsea because there was a lot of disruption one way and another. But once things settled down a bit I really enjoyed myself playing in midfield. I felt much more involved than when I played at full-back and I think it could be my best position in the long run.

But when the season ended, Chelsea hadn't won anything and I had to look elsewhere to celebrate success. And there was plenty of it going on in the north-east of England because as well as Scarborough's elevation to League status, my old club Middlesbrough won promotion from the Third as local rivals Sunderland were relegated from the Second.

Obviously my main priority this season is to win something with Chelsea but I will always have half an eye on the fortunes of my home town club Scarborough. I just hope they become a successful League club, which I'm sure they could be with my dad as chairman. Having been a player himself, he knows just what is needed throughout the club. And of course if he needs any scouting done in the London area, I'm sure he'll be on the phone to me!

I'll be happy to help out as long as it doesn't disrupt my own career too much. I wouldn't want to become a full-time scout, while I've hopefully got a lot of time left as a player.

# IT'S A FUNNY GAME

WE'LL PLAY WITH THE TELEVISION CAMERAS FACING US!

BUSY DOWN YOUR END?

HEY, REF — I THOUGHT YOU WERE CLAMPING DOWN ON TACKLING FROM BEHIND?

MISTER, CAN WE HAVE OUR BALL BACK?

HE'S A TERRIBLE PLAYER— BUT HE INJURES WELL!

NOW THERE'S SOMETHING YOU DON'T SEE EVERY SATURDAY!

## IT HAPPENED LAST SEASON (P113)

### ANSWERS

**1.** Eric Nixon (Manchester City) on loan to Southampton (First Division), Bradford City (Second), Carlisle United (Third) and Wolves (Fourth). **2.** Andy Jones (Port Vale). **3.** Chelsea. **4.** Adrian Sprott. **5.** Northampton Town. **6.** Blackburn Rovers. **7.** Kevin Ratcliffe. **8.** Billy Abercromby (St. Mirren). **9.** Alan Smith (Leicester to Arsenal), Clive Wilson (Manchester City to Chelsea) and Richard Hill (Northampton to Watford). **10.** Norwich City at Carrow Road. **11.** Ian Snodin. Leeds United to Everton for £840,000. **12.** Brian McClair (Celtic). 36 goals. **13.** 49 goals. **14.** Northampton Town. 103 goals. **15.** Lincoln City. **16.** Rangers' Chris Woods didn't concede a goal between November 29 and February 7. **17.** Oldham Athletic. **18.** Gary Plumley (Watford). **19.** Tony Cottee (West Ham), Tony Adams (Arsenal) and Stuart Pearce (Nottingham Forest).

## CROSSWORD (P100)

| ¹H | ²A | M | | ³L | I | ⁴N | E | K | E | ⁵R |
|----|----|----|----|----|----|----|----|----|----|----|
| O | | A | | I | | E | | | | I |
| ⁶M | O | R | A | N | | ⁷W | A | S | P | S |
| E | | I | | E | | E | | | | K |
| ⁸R | I | N | G | | ⁹C | L | E | ¹⁰E | A | R | S |
| | | E | | ¹¹D | | L | | I | | |
| ¹²P | A | R | K | E | S | | | R | | ¹³A |
| L | | | | A | | | | D | | L |
| ¹⁴A | L | L | ¹⁵E | N | | ¹⁶D | U | R | I | E |
| C | | | E | | | | | E | | I |
| ¹⁷E | V | E | R | T | O | N | | E | | T |

124

# Your Picture Index

## COLOUR PIN-UPS ACTION

Printed and published in Great Britain by D.C. THOMSON & CO., LTD., 185 Fleet Street, London EC4A 2HS.
© D.C. THOMSON & CO., LTD., 1987.
**ISBN** 0 85116 406 4

# Merry Christmas!

**How clubs up and
down the country w
one another well**

. . . From Arsenal.

. . . From Grimsby Town.

. . . From Southampton.

. . . From Stockport County

. . . From Hibernian.

Merry Christmas